1990

THE CONDITION OF THE PROFESSORIATE

1990

A TECHNICAL REPORT

The Condition of the Professoriate

ATTITUDES AND TRENDS, 1989

WITH A FOREWORD BY

ERNEST L. BOYER

THE CARNEGIE FOUNDATION FOR THE
ADVANCEMENT OF TEACHING

5 IVY LANE, PRINCETON, NEW JERSEY 08540

Library of Congress Cataloging-in-Publication Data

The Condition of the professoriate : attitudes and trends, 1989 : a
    technical report / with a foreword by Ernest L. Boyer.
        p.   cm.
    ISBN 0-931050-37-5 : $12.00
    1. College teachers—United States—Attitudes—Evaluation.
2. College teachers—United States—Statistics. 3. Education,
Higher—United States—Evaluation. 4. Education,
Higher—United States—Statistics. I. Carnegie Foundation for
the Advancement of Teaching.
LB1778.C628   1989
378. 1'2'0973021—dc20   89-28921
                                                     CIP

Copies are available from the
PRINCETON UNIVERSITY PRESS
3175 Princeton Pike
Lawrenceville, New Jersey 08648

CONTENTS

TABLES   vii

CHARTS   xv

FOREWORD BY ERNEST L. BOYER   xix

1.   *The Goals of Collegiate Education*   1

2.   *Academic Standards*   17

3.   *Attitudes About Student Life*   33

4.   *Teaching, Research, and Service*   41

5.   *Status of the Profession*   69

6.   *Views of the Institution*   93

7.   *Participation in Decision-making*   129

8.   *General Observations*   137

APPENDIX A: *Technical Notes*   145

APPENDIX B: *Carnegie Classifications*   147

TABLES

Number	Title	Page
1	Undergraduate education in America would be improved if there were less emphasis on specialized training and more on broad liberal education	2
2	The number of general education courses required of all undergraduates should be increased	3
3	Apart from major field requirements, undergraduates should be required to take which of the following?	4
4	How important is it to enhance creative thinking in undergraduate education?	5
5	How important is it to provide a basic understanding of mathematics and science in undergraduate education?	6
6	How important is it to provide knowledge of history and the social sciences in undergraduate education?	7
7	How important is it to provide an appreciation of literature and the arts in undergraduate education?	8
8	How important is it to shape student values in undergraduate education?	9
9	How important is it to provide knowledge of one subject in depth in undergraduate education?	10
10	How important is it to prepare students for a career?	11
11	Undergraduates have become more careerist in their concerns	12

Number	Title	Page
12	Too many students ill-suited to academic life are now enrolling in colleges and universities	18
13	The undergraduates with whom I have close contact are seriously under-prepared in basic skills	19
14	This institution spends too much time and money teaching students what they should have learned in high school	20
15	On the whole, undergraduates are now more willing to work hard in their studies	21
16	Most undergraduates at my institution only do enough to get by	22
17	Grade inflation is a problem at my institution	23
18	Undergraduates today are more competitive academically	24
19	Undergraduates have become more grade conscious	25
20	Today's undergraduates are more willing to cheat in order to get good grades	26
21	There has been a widespread lowering of standards in American higher education	27
22	Academic standards for undergraduate admissions at my institution should be . . .	28
23	Academic standards for bachelor's degrees at my institution should be . . .	29
24	Undergraduates have become more conservative in lifestyle	34

Number	Title	Page
25	Undergraduates have become more conservative politically	35
26	There is more alcohol abuse among today's undergraduates than five years ago	36
27	There is more drug abuse among today's undergraduates than five years ago	37
28	There is more violence and crime perpetrated by off-campus criminals now	38
29	There is a growing trend among undergraduates to isolate themselves in small groups	39
30	Do your interests lie primarily in research or in teaching?	43
31	In my undergraduate courses, I prefer teaching students who have a clear idea of the career they will be following	44
32	Teaching effectiveness should be the primary criterion for promotion of faculty	45
33	How important are student evaluations of courses for granting tenure in your department?	46
34	Are you currently engaged in any scholarly work that you expect to lead to a publication, an exhibit, or a musical recital?	47
35	In my department it is difficult for a person to achieve tenure if he or she does not publish	48
36	How important is the number of publications for granting tenure in your department?	49

Number	Title	Page
37	At my institution publications used for tenure and promotion are just counted, not qualitatively measured	50
38	The pressure to publish reduces the quality of teaching at my university	51
39	At my institution we need better ways, besides publications, to evaluate the scholarly performance of the faculty	52
40	The undergraduate curriculum has suffered from the specialization of faculty members	53
41	How important to you is your relationship with undergraduates?	54
42	Undergraduates should seek out faculty only during posted office hours	55
43	I enjoy interacting informally with undergraduates outside the classroom	56
44	Fewer faculty members provide positive role models to our undergraduates than in the past	57
45	During the past 12 months, did you receive research support from federal agencies?	58
46	During the past 12 months, did you receive research support from institutional or departmental funds?	59
47	During the past two years, have you served as a paid or unpaid consultant to a private business or industry?	60
48	During the past two years, have you served as a paid or unpaid consultant to schools (elementary or secondary)?	61
49	Faculty members in high schools and colleges should work together to improve education in my discipline	62

x

Number	Title	Page
50	Exciting developments are now taking place in my discipline	71
51	In my discipline, most faculty agree on the standards of good scholarship	72
52	This is a poor time for any young person to begin an academic career	73
53	How have job prospects for undergraduates in your field changed over the past five years?	74
54	If I had it to do over again, I would not become a college teacher	75
55	I am more enthusiastic about my work now than when I began my academic career	76
56	I often wish I had entered another profession	77
57	During the past two years, have you ever considered a permanent departure from academia?	78
58	I feel trapped in a profession with limited opportunities for advancement	79
59	I tend to subordinate all aspects of my life to my work	80
60	I hardly ever get time to give a piece of work the attention it deserves	81
61	My job is the source of considerable personal strain	82
62	How would you rate your own salary?	83
63	On the whole, faculty salaries here have kept up with the rate of inflation	84
64	During the past two or three years, financial support for work in my discipline has become harder to obtain	85

Number	Title	Page
65	I would exercise an early retirement option if it were offered to me	86
66	I look forward to retirement as an enjoyable period of my life	87
67	In general, how do you feel about your institution?	95
68	The administration here supports academic freedom	96
69	Undergraduates at my institution are not getting as good an education as they did five years ago	97
70	Rate the performance of your institution in providing undergraduates with a general education	98
71	Rate the performance of your institution in preparing undergraduates for a career	99
72	Rate the performance of your institution in providing undergraduates with the opportunity to explore a subject in depth	100
73	Rate the performance of your institution in strengthening the values of undergraduates	101
74	Rate the performance of your institution in creating opportunities for undergraduates to engage in public service	102
75	In the next five years, I expect that some of the tenured faculty here will lose their jobs due to lack of funds	103
76	Many young faculty members at this institution will leave because it is tenured in	104
77	I am satisfied with the results of affirmative action at this institution	105

Number	Title	Page
78	My institution provides the conditions and support for faculty to retire with dignity	106
79	How would you rate the administration at your institution?	107
80	Do you feel that the administration of your institution is autocratic or democratic?	108
81	There are more part-time and adjunct faculty members at this institution today than there were five years ago	109
82	In my department tenure is now more difficult to achieve than it was five years ago	110
83	My institution is managed effectively	111
84	My institution has serious financial problems	112
85	How would you rate the quality of life at your institution?	113
86	How would you rate the intellectual environment at your institution?	114
87	How would you rate the sense of community at your institution?	115
88	How important to you is your college or university?	116
89	How important to you is your academic discipline?	117
90	How important to you is your department?	118
91	How important to you are national or international societies in your discipline?	119

Number	Title	Page
92	How has departmental morale changed over the past five years?	120
93	How much opportunity do you have to influence the policies of your institution?	130
94	How much opportunity do you have to influence the policies of your department?	131
95	Indicate the extent to which you participate in departmental faculty meetings at your institution	132
96	Indicate the extent to which you participate in campus-wide faculty committee meetings at your institution	133
97	Indicate the extent to which you participate in faculty senate (or comparable campus-wide faculty unit) meetings at your institution	134
98	Indicate the extent to which you participate in administrative advisory committee meetings at your institution	135
99	I am apprehensive about the future of this country	138
100	I am less confident today than I used to be about the capacities of higher education to help make a better society	139
101	The United States is creating an overtrained work force in terms of available jobs	140
102	Performing sponsored research for a private company is not a proper university activity	141
103	The abolition of faculty tenure would, on the whole, improve the quality of American higher education	142
104	How would you characterize yourself politically at the present time?	143

C H A R T S

Number	Title	Page
1	Undergraduates should have less specialized training and more broad liberal education	13
2	Undergraduates should be required to take a common core	14
3	Undergraduates should be required to take breadth requirements	14
4	Undergraduate education: importance of enhancing creative thinking	15
5	Undergraduate education: importance of providing appreciation for literature and the arts	15
6	Undergraduate education: importance of shaping students' values	16
7	Undergraduate education: importance of preparing students for a career	16
8	This institution spends too much time and money teaching students what they should have learned in high school	30
9	Academic standards for undergraduate admissions should be higher	31
10	Academic standards for bachelor's degrees should be higher	31
11	My interests lie primarily in or leaning toward teaching	63
12	Prefer teaching students with a clear idea of their career	64
13	Teaching effectiveness should be the primary criterion for promotion	64
14	It is difficult for a person to receive tenure if he/she does not publish	65

Number	Title	Page
15	Undergraduate curriculum has suffered from specialization of faculty	65
16	Undergraduates should seek out faculty only during posted office hours	66
17	Received research support in last 12 months from federal agencies	66
18	Received research support in last 12 months from institutional funds	67
19	Served as a consultant to private business or industry in last two years	67
20	This is a poor time for any young person to begin an academic career	88
21	If deciding again, I would not become a college teacher	89
22	I tend to subordinate all aspects of life to my work	89
23	I hardly ever get time to give a piece of work the attention it deserves	90
24	My job is the source of considerable personal strain	90
25	Would you rate your own salary as excellent or good?	91
26	Faculty salaries have kept up with the rate of inflation	91
27	In general, my institution is a very good place	121
28	Performance of institution in providing undergraduates with general education	122
29	Performance of institution in preparing undergraduates for a career	122
30	Some faculty will lose jobs due to lack of funds	123
31	Administration at your institution is fair or poor	123

Number	Title	Page
32	Administration of institution is somewhat or very autocratic	124
33	Tenure is more difficult to achieve than five years ago	124
34	This institution has serious financial problems	125
35	Intellectual environment at your institution is fair or poor	125
36	How important to you is your college or university?	126
37	How important to you is your academic discipline?	126
38	How important to you is your department?	127
39	How has departmental morale changed over the past five years?	127
40	I am apprehensive about the future of this country	144

FOREWORD

by Ernest L. Boyer

From the very first, The Carnegie Foundation for the Advancement of Teaching has had an abiding interest in the status of college faculty. The Foundation began in 1905 with the goal of easing financial hardship among retired professors, but that specific purpose quickly broadened into a more general one about the condition of the professoriate overall. We have never lost sight of that concern.

To underscore our commitment to college teaching, the Foundation has, over the years, conducted a series of surveys that has helped to clarify the status of the professoriate and, in a larger sense, provide a portrait of American higher education.

Early in 1989, the Foundation gathered information from more than 5,000 faculty members at all types of higher learning institutions. We included many questions asked before, as well as a series of new ones about campus community, students, tenure, and retirement. We have organized the findings of our most recent survey in the following eight areas:

- the goals of collegiate education
- academic standards
- attitudes about student life
- teaching, research, and service
- status of the profession
- views of the institution
- participation in decision-making
- general observations

Further, because of variation in faculty attitudes, we have organized the data in the tables that follow on the basis of age, gender, professional discipline, and institutional type. In addition, we occasionally present data gathered in our prior surveys to show trendlines.

Three issues emerged in this, our fourth national survey, that vividly define the optimism, as well as the concerns, of the professoriate today.

The first issue relates to academic quality. We found that since 1984, the faculty have dramatically confirmed their commitment to liberal learning. A majority of faculty also feel students should study a core of general education subjects, and they believe that "becoming proficient in creative thinking" is the most important goal of undergraduate education.

Faculty are increasingly optimistic about their own profession. We found, for example, that two-thirds feel this is a good time for a young person to begin an academic career, and about half believe that in the last five years job prospects in their field have gotten better. Only 12 percent conclude they've gotten worse. In addition, 77 percent of today's professors say that "if I had it to do over again, I would become a college teacher."

Three out of four faculty also believe that their college is providing above-average general education for its students and is doing a good job of preparing students for careers. A majority also report that students are being provided a good opportunity to explore a subject in depth. All of this suggests a robust condition within the professoriate.

On the darker side, today's faculty present a discouraging portrait of students, both in the classroom and beyond. At the very time professors are calling for more liberal education, 84 percent report that undergraduates at their institution have become more careerist in their concerns.

Even more troublesome, about two-thirds of the faculty say that too many students are ill-prepared for academic life, and they conclude that their institution spends too much time and money teaching students what they should have learned in high school.

Faculty also feel that grade inflation is a serious problem at their institution, and by a two-to-one margin they believe that today's students are more willing to cheat in order to get good grades. While most faculty feel *their* college offers a good education, they also conclude that, overall, there has been a "widespread lowering of standards in higher education." It's not surprising, therefore, that most believe that both admission *and* graduation standards should be raised.

Beyond this, faculty expressing an opinion report that there is more alcohol and drug abuse among students, more violence on campus, and a growing trend among undergraduates to isolate in small groups.

Thus, professors have deepened their commitment to liberal learning. They are optimistic about prospects in their profession, and they appear to be quite satisfied with the quality of undergraduate education at their own institution. But they judge negatively the academic preparation of students and the quality of student life outside the classroom.

Faculty have always been less than fully satisfied about the academic seriousness of their students, but trendlines reported here reinforce the fact that colleges can be no stronger than the nation's schools, and that public education, despite six years of reform, is still producing inadequately prepared students.

We conclude that college professors should join with colleagues in the schools to strengthen academic standards, focusing especially on the writing proficiency of students. We commend the National Writing Project and other school partnerships, and we're encouraged that over 80 percent of those responding to our survey agreed that faculty members should work with surrounding schools to improve education. Acting on this commitment is essential, if quality in higher education is to be achieved.

The second major issue relates to teaching and research. Over 70 percent of today's faculty say that their interests lie in teaching, and a significant percentage also conclude that "teaching effectiveness should be the primary criterion for promotion." Further, faculty overwhelmingly say they enjoy interacting informally with undergraduates *outside* the classroom, and most reject the notion that students should seek faculty help *only* during posted office hours. Clearly, the majority of faculty consider teaching to be a central mission and enjoy the time they spend with students.

But most faculty at the four-year institutions also report that the reward system is heavily weighted toward published research, not effective teaching, and more than one-third of faculty support the proposition that at their institutions, publications are "just counted, not qualitatively measured." Even at research universities, a surprising 42 percent agree with this conclusion.

The irony is that while pressures for research and publication keep going up, faculty report that federal and institutional support for such activity is going down.

Research is essential to American higher education. Now, more than ever, scholars must discover new knowledge and advance the frontiers of their field. Therefore, funding for basic research should be expanded, not diminished. But, the nation's colleges and universities enroll, every year, over 12 million students of great diversity and in so doing, accept a profoundly important obligation also to promote excellence in teaching.

What we need, then, in higher education is a reward system that reflects the diversity of our institutions and the breadth of scholarship, as well. The challenge is to strike a balance among teaching, research, and service, a position supported by two-thirds of today's faculty who conclude that, "at my institution, we need better ways, besides publication, to evaluate scholarly performance of faculty."

The third issue is how faculty feel about the institution where they work. It's significant, we believe, that over 90 percent of today's faculty say their institution is a "very good" or "fairly good" place to work, and most agree that the administration at their college or university supports academic freedom. We also are impressed that the percentage of faculty who feel their institution is "very important" to them has increased since 1984, from 29 to 40 percent.

Further, in spite of the deficiencies of undergraduates in American higher education, most faculty believe that students at their institution are getting as good an education as they did five years ago.

Faculty also seem to feel quite good about the degree to which they participate in decision-making on campus. For example, 69 percent say they have an opportunity to influence, at least somewhat, policies at their institutions; within their departments, it's 96 percent. Well over 90 percent of the faculty say they participate in departmental meetings, while over 40 percent report participating in campus-wide meetings of the senate. In general, then, American professors believe they at least have some control over professional decisions that affect their lives.

But we also found that, once again, about two-thirds of today's faculty rate the administration at their campus as either "fair" or "poor." Even more disturbing, 69 percent feel that their administration is "autocratic." The exception is the liberal arts college, where faculty view campus leaders as being somewhat more "democratic."

Faculty evaluate their institutions rather negatively in other ways as well. For example, only half feel their college or university is managed effectively, and in significant numbers, they rate the intellectual environment and the sense of community on campus as either "fair" or "poor."

How, then, should these somewhat contradictory patterns of opinion be interpreted? The negative feelings faculty have about administrators may relate, at least in part, to the size of the institution, since liberal arts and two-year college faculty are more generous in their ratings. As bureaucracy grows, faculty frequently are more removed from decision-making on campus. Full information about complicated issues becomes more difficult to disseminate, and those who make campus-wide decisions, appear, from afar, to be autocratic.

Further, colleges and universities feel pressures to cut costs and tighten administrative control, while, at the same time trying to satisfy competing interests. In such a climate, it's understandable that faculty feel at times that their particular concerns are not adequately supported.

If the college or university is to be a community of learning, effective governance is essential. Better forums are needed to address common educational questions, so that credibility in the decision-making process can be strengthened. Without such arrangements, the institution drifts, larger purposes are blurred, and the unity of the higher learning enterprise is lost.

Despite the tensions, we believe the American professoriate is, today, in a healthier state than it was five years ago. We found in our survey a feeling of optimism among professors about their disciplines and a renewed commitment to liberal learning. We also found that faculty feel quite satisfied in some important ways about the places where they work.

At the same time, we cannot overstate our sense of urgency about the problems faculty have defined—the decline of academic standards among students, the ambivalence they feel about teaching and research, and the lack of confidence they have in campus leadership. How the academy confronts these essential issues surely will shape the quality of higher education for years to come.

The Goals of Collegiate Education

In their response to the Carnegie survey, the nation's faculty express an impressive commitment to liberal education. There is widespread agreement on the fundamental goals of an undergraduate education, and a majority of faculty believe this education would be improved if there were more emphasis on broad liberal learning and less on specialized training. It is interesting to note that the number of faculty who support this view has been growing since 1975.

At the same time, faculty are less certain about how to translate a commitment to liberal education into curricular improvements. While the majority of faculty believe undergraduates should take either a common core or breadth requirements, only 37 percent conclude that the number of general education courses required of undergraduates should be increased. Core courses are a slight favorite, but they have declined in popularity since 1984, while breadth requirements have increased. Obviously, faculty feel that requirements are essential to an undergraduate education: only 1 percent believe there should be none at all.

While creative thinking has long been one of the most important goals faculty promote in an undergraduate education, it now rates above all others. Indeed, the number of faculty who consider it very important has increased sharply in the past five years. Comments that faculty made to us on our survey suggest that the change is rooted in their classroom experience. As one professor put it, "For our students, abstract thinking is very difficult." Another remarked, "We need to work to re-emphasize thinking and creativity in students."

Faculty also rate other goals highly. A majority believe it is very important to provide a basic understanding of math and science, knowledge of history and the social sciences, and an appreciation of literature and the arts. More than 40 percent of the professors we surveyed believe that shaping student values is also a very important part of an undergraduate education.

In light of their commitment to liberal goals in education, it is unsurprising that faculty consider career training a lower priority in undergraduate experience. Less than a third believe that providing knowledge of one subject in depth or preparing students for a career is very important. In fact, the number of professors who feel that career preparation is very important has been declining since 1975.

Further, faculty register their continuing concern about what they believe is inordinate careerism among today's undergraduates. Overwhelmingly, faculty report that students are more careerist in their concerns. This creates, potentially, a troubling tension on campus, with student and faculty interests moving in opposite directions.

Table 1

Undergraduate Education in America Would Be Improved If There Were Less Emphasis on Specialized Training and More on Broad Liberal Education

	AGREE	NEUTRAL	DISAGREE
ALL FACULTY	**56%**	**16%**	**27%**
TYPE OF INSTITUTION			
Four Year	58	16	26
Two Year	54	15	31
CARNEGIE CLASSIFICATION			
Research	56	18	26
Doctorate	56	16	28
Comprehensive	59	15	26
Liberal Arts	68	15	17
Two Year	54	15	31
AGE			
Under 40	52	18	29
40 to 49	57	15	28
50 to 59	56	16	29
60 to 64	61	16	23
65 and over	62	16	22
GENDER			
Male	56	15	28
Female	57	18	25
DEPARTMENT			
Biological Sciences	55	18	28
Business/Communications	50	16	34
Education	52	22	26
Engineering	19	13	68
Humanities	79	10	11
Mathematics	44	28	28
Physical Sciences	47	20	34
Social Sciences	71	16	13
Other	36	19	45

Table 2

The Number of General Education Courses Required of All Undergraduates Should Be Increased

	AGREE	NEUTRAL	DISAGREE
ALL FACULTY	**37%**	**23%**	**39%**
TYPE OF INSTITUTION			
Four Year	36	25	39
Two Year	41	21	39
CARNEGIE CLASSIFICATION			
Research	40	28	33
Doctorate	33	27	40
Comprehensive	34	22	44
Liberal Arts	33	21	46
Two Year	41	21	39
AGE			
Under 40	37	25	38
40 to 49	38	24	38
50 to 59	36	21	43
60 to 64	37	22	40
65 and over	40	27	33
GENDER			
Male	37	24	39
Female	38	22	39
DEPARTMENT			
Biological Sciences	31	25	43
Business/Communications	36	20	44
Education	35	25	40
Engineering	26	20	54
Humanities	47	20	34
Mathematics	40	27	34
Physical Sciences	30	31	39
Social Sciences	41	24	35
Other	31	26	43

Table 3

Apart from Major Field Requirements, Undergraduates Should Be Required to Take Which of the Following?

	REQUIRED COMMON CORE	BREADTH REQUIREMENTS	NO REQUIRED COURSES	PUBLIC SERVICE INTERNSHIP	NO OPINION
ALL FACULTY	**47%**	**43%**	**1%**	**2%**	**6%**
TYPE OF INSTITUTION					
Four Year	48	43	2	2	5
Two Year	46	44	1	2	7
CARNEGIE CLASSIFICATION					
Research	44	44	2	2	8
Doctorate	54	35	2	3	7
Comprehensive	48	46	1	2	3
Liberal Arts	54	38	2	3	3
Two Year	46	44	1	2	7
AGE					
Under 40	42	45	2	4	7
40 to 49	49	42	1	3	5
50 to 59	50	41	1	2	5
60 to 64	43	47	1	1	7
65 and over	43	46	1	1	9
GENDER					
Male	48	42	2	2	6
Female	46	45	1	3	5
DEPARTMENT					
Biological Sciences	44	51	1	1	2
Business/Communications	50	41	2	1	6
Education	45	40	1	7	7
Engineering	46	31	5	1	17
Humanities	49	45	1	2	3
Mathematics	48	38	2	1	11
Physical Sciences	45	45	3	0	6
Social Sciences	44	47	0	3	5
Other	48	41	1	3	7

Table 4

How Important Is It to Enhance
Creative Thinking in Undergraduate Education?

	VERY IMPORTANT	FAIRLY IMPORTANT	FAIRLY UNIMPORTANT	VERY UNIMPORTANT	NO OPINION
ALL FACULTY	**70%**	**26%**	**2%**	**0%**	**1%**
TYPE OF INSTITUTION					
Four Year	72	25	2	1	1
Two Year	67	30	3	0	0
CARNEGIE CLASSIFICATION					
Research	72	25	1	1	1
Doctorate	73	24	2	0	1
Comprehensive	71	25	3	1	0
Liberal Arts	79	20	1	0	0
Two Year	67	30	3	0	0
AGE					
Under 40	73	25	2	0	0
40 to 49	71	27	1	0	0
50 to 59	69	27	3	1	0
60 to 64	69	27	3	0	1
65 and over	67	24	5	1	3
GENDER					
Male	69	27	2	1	1
Female	73	24	2	0	0
DEPARTMENT					
Biological Sciences	79	20	1	0	0
Business/Communications	68	28	2	1	1
Education	63	31	2	1	3
Engineering	65	34	1	0	0
Humanities	75	22	3	0	0
Mathematics	61	36	3	0	0
Physical Sciences	68	29	2	0	1
Social Sciences	70	25	3	1	1
Other	69	28	3	0	0

Table 5

How Important Is It to Provide a Basic Understanding of Mathematics and Science in Undergraduate Education?

	VERY IMPORTANT	FAIRLY IMPORTANT	FAIRLY UNIMPORTANT	VERY UNIMPORTANT	NO OPINION
ALL FACULTY	**59%**	**37%**	**3%**	**0%**	**1%**
TYPE OF INSTITUTION					
Four Year	59	37	3	0	1
Two Year	59	37	3	1	1
CARNEGIE CLASSIFICATION					
Research	59	37	3	0	1
Doctorate	59	38	2	0	1
Comprehensive	58	38	3	0	1
Liberal Arts	62	35	2	1	0
Two Year	59	37	3	1	1
AGE					
Under 40	60	36	3	1	0
40 to 49	60	38	2	0	1
50 to 59	56	39	4	1	1
60 to 64	62	35	2	0	1
65 and over	67	30	3	0	0
GENDER					
Male	57	39	3	0	1
Female	64	33	2	1	1
DEPARTMENT					
Biological Sciences	71	28	1	0	0
Business/Communications	53	44	1	1	1
Education	51	42	3	1	3
Engineering	66	31	3	0	0
Humanities	58	37	4	0	1
Mathematics	72	27	1	0	0
Physical Sciences	68	31	1	0	0
Social Sciences	57	40	2	0	1
Other	56	39	4	1	0

Table 6

How Important Is It to Provide Knowledge of History and the Social Sciences in Undergraduate Education?

	VERY IMPORTANT	FAIRLY IMPORTANT	FAIRLY UNIMPORTANT	VERY UNIMPORTANT	NO OPINION
ALL FACULTY	**52%**	**42%**	**5%**	**1%**	**1%**
TYPE OF INSTITUTION					
Four Year	53	41	4	1	1
Two Year	50	42	6	1	0
CARNEGIE CLASSIFICATION					
Research	53	41	5	0	1
Doctorate	52	42	5	1	0
Comprehensive	52	42	4	1	1
Liberal Arts	59	39	1	0	0
Two Year	50	42	6	1	0
AGE					
Under 40	46	47	6	1	1
40 to 49	54	40	5	0	1
50 to 59	51	43	4	1	1
60 to 64	58	39	3	0	1
65 and over	58	34	3	3	1
GENDER					
Male	50	43	5	1	1
Female	57	38	3	1	0
DEPARTMENT					
Biological Sciences	50	43	7	1	0
Business/Communications	43	51	5	1	0
Education	54	39	2	2	3
Engineering	27	50	16	5	2
Humanities	67	32	1	0	0
Mathematics	48	45	5	2	0
Physical Sciences	47	48	4	1	1
Social Sciences	62	36	1	0	1
Other	41	47	10	0	1

Table 7

How Important Is It to Provide an Appreciation of Literature and the Arts in Undergraduate Education?

	VERY IMPORTANT	FAIRLY IMPORTANT	FAIRLY UNIMPORTANT	VERY UNIMPORTANT	NO OPINION
ALL FACULTY	**50%**	**41%**	**7%**	**1%**	**1%**
TYPE OF INSTITUTION					
Four Year	53	39	6	1	1
Two Year	44	44	10	1	1
CARNEGIE CLASSIFICATION					
Research	53	39	7	1	1
Doctorate	50	41	7	1	1
Comprehensive	52	40	6	1	1
Liberal Arts	65	32	2	1	0
Two Year	44	44	10	1	1
AGE					
Under 40	42	47	10	1	1
40 to 49	50	41	7	1	1
50 to 59	52	39	6	2	0
60 to 64	59	34	6	1	0
65 and over	50	38	8	0	3
GENDER					
Male	48	41	8	1	1
Female	54	39	5	1	1
DEPARTMENT					
Biological Sciences	41	50	8	1	1
Business/Communications	36	51	10	3	0
Education	50	38	8	1	3
Engineering	23	50	20	6	1
Humanities	78	21	1	0	0
Mathematics	39	48	8	4	1
Physical Sciences	42	50	6	0	2
Social Sciences	50	46	3	1	1
Other	39	45	14	1	1

Table 8

How Important Is It to Shape
Student Values in Undergraduate Education?

	VERY IMPORTANT	FAIRLY IMPORTANT	FAIRLY UNIMPORTANT	VERY UNIMPORTANT	NO OPINION
ALL FACULTY	**41%**	**44%**	**10%**	**3%**	**2%**
TYPE OF INSTITUTION					
Four Year	40	43	11	3	3
Two Year	43	46	8	2	2
CARNEGIE CLASSIFICATION					
Research	37	41	15	4	3
Doctorate	39	42	12	3	4
Comprehensive	40	47	8	2	3
Liberal Arts	54	37	6	2	2
Two Year	43	46	8	2	2
AGE					
Under 40	38	43	13	3	2
40 to 49	39	46	9	3	3
50 to 59	43	44	9	2	2
60 to 64	52	37	8	2	2
65 and over	43	40	13	2	1
GENDER					
Male	39	45	11	3	2
Female	46	42	7	2	3
DEPARTMENT					
Biological Sciences	40	43	12	2	3
Business/Communications	43	42	11	3	2
Education	35	47	11	3	4
Engineering	42	46	8	1	3
Humanities	51	40	5	2	1
Mathematics	32	43	18	7	0
Physical Sciences	32	47	13	3	4
Social Sciences	31	50	12	4	3
Other	43	44	9	1	3

Table 9

How Important Is It to Provide Knowledge
of One Subject in Depth in Undergraduate Education?

	VERY IMPORTANT	FAIRLY IMPORTANT	FAIRLY UNIMPORTANT	VERY UNIMPORTANT	NO OPINION
ALL FACULTY	**32%**	**46%**	**15%**	**5%**	**2%**
TYPE OF INSTITUTION					
Four Year	35	46	13	4	1
Two Year	27	45	17	8	4
CARNEGIE CLASSIFICATION					
Research	32	45	16	5	2
Doctorate	34	48	13	4	2
Comprehensive	37	47	11	4	1
Liberal Arts	38	46	12	4	1
Two Year	27	45	17	8	4
AGE					
Under 40	31	49	15	3	2
40 to 49	30	48	15	6	2
50 to 59	33	44	14	6	2
60 to 64	37	41	11	7	4
65 and over	34	40	18	4	5
GENDER					
Male	31	46	15	6	2
Female	34	46	13	5	2
DEPARTMENT					
Biological Sciences	36	43	13	5	3
Business/Communications	27	49	15	5	3
Education	38	45	11	3	3
Engineering	33	47	16	4	0
Humanities	35	42	15	7	1
Mathematics	29	54	11	2	4
Physical Sciences	43	43	11	2	2
Social Sciences	23	48	19	6	4
Other	33	46	14	5	2

Table 10

How Important Is It to Prepare Students for a Career?

	VERY IMPORTANT	FAIRLY IMPORTANT	FAIRLY UNIMPORTANT	VERY UNIMPORTANT	NO OPINION
ALL FACULTY	**31%**	**44%**	**19%**	**5%**	**1%**
TYPE OF INSTITUTION					
Four Year	23	46	23	7	1
Two Year	47	40	11	2	1
CARNEGIE CLASSIFICATION					
Research	19	42	27	10	1
Doctorate	24	47	21	5	2
Comprehensive	27	48	18	6	1
Liberal Arts	23	45	24	6	1
Two Year	47	40	11	2	1
AGE					
Under 40	34	39	21	5	1
40 to 49	28	44	20	7	1
50 to 59	30	48	16	5	1
60 to 64	35	44	18	2	1
65 and over	39	39	17	4	0
GENDER					
Male	28	45	21	6	1
Female	39	40	14	5	1
DEPARTMENT					
Biological Sciences	33	38	22	5	1
Business/Communications	38	45	11	4	1
Education	32	42	17	5	3
Engineering	41	42	15	1	0
Humanities	19	46	25	8	1
Mathematics	32	45	18	4	0
Physical Sciences	20	56	19	4	1
Social Sciences	17	45	27	9	1
Other	54	36	9	1	0

Table 11

Undergraduates Have Become More Careerist in Their Concerns

	AGREE	NEUTRAL	DISAGREE
ALL FACULTY	**84%**	**11%**	**5%**
TYPE OF INSTITUTION			
Four Year	86	10	3
Two Year	79	13	8
CARNEGIE CLASSIFICATION			
Research	85	12	3
Doctorate	87	10	3
Comprehensive	87	9	4
Liberal Arts	89	8	4
Two Year	79	13	8
AGE			
Under 40	88	8	4
40 to 49	84	11	5
50 to 59	84	11	5
60 to 64	79	16	6
65 and over	76	16	8
GENDER			
Male	84	11	4
Female	82	12	6
DEPARTMENT			
Biological Sciences	87	9	4
Business/Communications	80	11	9
Education	84	13	3
Engineering	70	22	7
Humanities	91	6	3
Mathematics	76	20	4
Physical Sciences	86	11	3
Social Sciences	86	11	3
Other	79	14	7

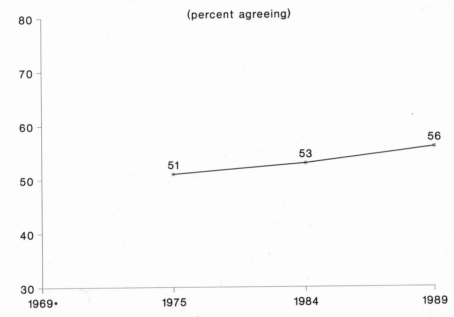

Chart 1. **Undergraduates Should Have Less Specialized Training and More Broad Liberal Education**

(percent agreeing)

•Data not available

13

Chart 2. **Undergraduates Should Be Required to Take a Common Core**

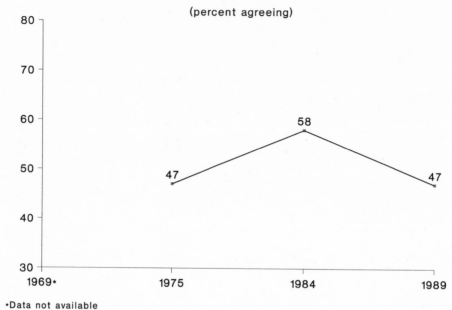

(percent agreeing)

*Data not available

Chart 3. **Undergraduates Should Be Required to Take Breadth Requirements**

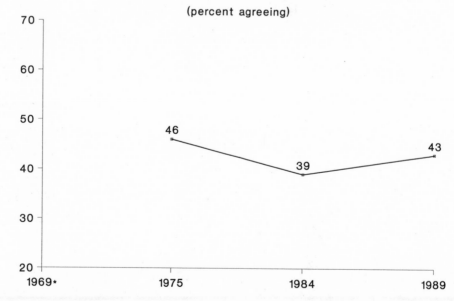

(percent agreeing)

*Data not available

14

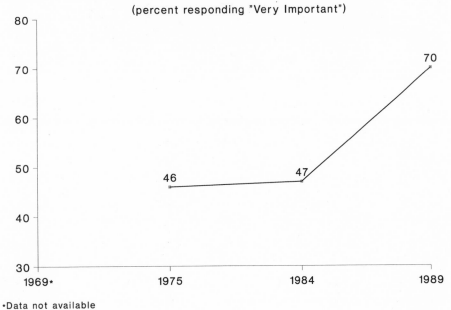

Chart 4. **Undergraduate Education: Importance of Enhancing Creative Thinking**

(percent responding "Very Important")

*Data not available

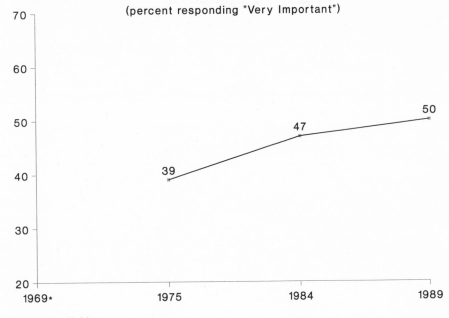

Chart 5. **Undergraduate Education: Importance of Providing Appreciation for Literature and the Arts**

(percent responding "Very Important")

*Data not available

Chart 6. **Undergraduate Education: Importance of Shaping Students' Values**

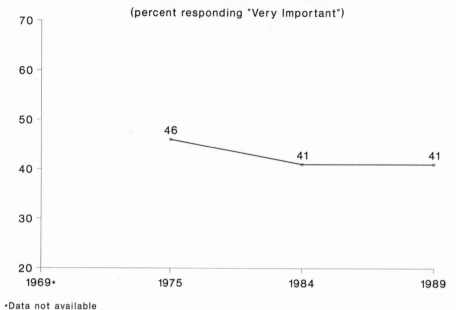

(percent responding "Very Important")

*Data not available

Chart 7. **Undergraduate Education: Importance of Preparing Students for a Career**

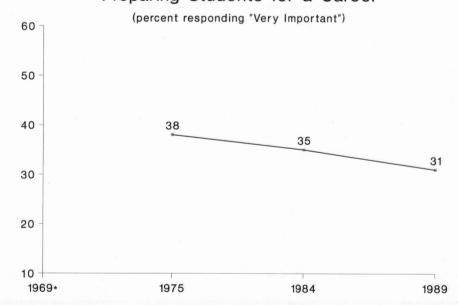

(percent responding "Very Important")

*Data not available

2

Academic Standards

Faculty are concerned that academic standards in higher education are eroding. Indeed, faculty feel that the students in their classrooms have not achieved the learning they need to succeed in higher education. Specifically, 64 percent of those we surveyed agree that too many students now enrolling in colleges are ill-suited to academic life, and three-quarters say that undergraduates with whom they have close contact are seriously underprepared in basic skills.

These opinions suggest that the nation's schools are, in fact, failing to equip students with the basic skills they need to pursue advanced degrees successfully. Thus, 68 percent of the faculty say their institution is spending too much time and money teaching students what they should have learned in high school. Despite the sustained efforts of education reformers to improve schools, the dissatisfaction of faculty remains unchanged from five years ago.

Especially revealing is the fact that professors feel students themselves contribute to the slackening of academic standards. A majority disagree with the idea that undergraduates are now more willing to work hard in their studies. Fifty-five percent suggest that most undergraduates do only enough to "get by."

At the same time, faculty themselves seem to take some responsibility for the decline in quality that they describe: 62 percent note that grade inflation is a problem at their institution. As one professor told us, "My institution has less grade inflation than most, but I have taught at supposedly prestigious schools where the students get away with murder. I have had students turn in unfinished papers (when I was a visiting professor elsewhere), knowing that the department gave out no grades lower than a B-."

Even as faculty describe students as less willing to work for a grade, they also describe them as more concerned about the grade they get. Some 42 percent say students are more competitive academically. A solid 70 percent say undergraduates have become more grade-conscious. Perhaps most disturbing is that a significant minority of the faculty say undergraduates are more willing to cheat to get good grades.

Taken together, these opinions paint a disturbing picture of academic quality. When faculty reflect upon the matter in general, two-thirds conclude that there has been a widespread lowering of standards in higher education. To correct the situation, professors would like to see more rigorous standards applied. Specifically, higher admission standards are suggested by 57 percent of all faculty, and the same number at four-year colleges would like to see higher standards for bachelor's degrees.

Table 12

Too Many Students Ill-suited to Academic Life
Are Now Enrolling in Colleges and Universities

	AGREE	NEUTRAL	DISAGREE
ALL FACULTY	**64%**	**13%**	**23%**
TYPE OF INSTITUTION			
Four Year	60	15	25
Two Year	70	10	21
CARNEGIE CLASSIFICATION			
Research	54	17	28
Doctorate	59	15	26
Comprehensive	66	13	21
Liberal Arts	61	12	27
Two Year	70	10	21
AGE			
Under 40	64	17	20
40 to 49	61	14	25
50 to 59	66	10	25
60 to 64	65	13	22
65 and over	64	16	21
GENDER			
Male	64	14	22
Female	63	10	27
DEPARTMENT			
Biological Sciences	63	13	23
Business/Communications	67	12	21
Education	40	20	40
Engineering	61	18	21
Humanities	65	10	25
Mathematics	72	9	20
Physical Sciences	73	12	15
Social Sciences	63	14	22
Other	60	15	25

18

Table 13

The Undergraduates with Whom I Have Close
Contact Are Seriously Underprepared in Basic Skills

	AGREE	NEUTRAL	DISAGREE
ALL FACULTY	**75%**	**9%**	**15%**
TYPE OF INSTITUTION			
Four Year	70	11	19
Two Year	85	7	8
CARNEGIE CLASSIFICATION			
Research	68	13	18
Doctorate	70	10	19
Comprehensive	73	9	18
Liberal Arts	64	8	28
Two Year	85	7	8
AGE			
Under 40	72	13	15
40 to 49	76	9	15
50 to 59	75	9	16
60 to 64	80	6	14
65 and over	76	6	18
GENDER			
Male	74	10	16
Female	77	9	14
DEPARTMENT			
Biological Sciences	75	7	18
Business/Communications	75	11	14
Education	50	21	28
Engineering	69	15	17
Humanities	79	7	15
Mathematics	80	10	10
Physical Sciences	72	13	15
Social Sciences	76	8	16
Other	79	8	13

Table 14

This Institution Spends Too Much Time and Money Teaching Students What They Should Have Learned in High School

	AGREE	NEUTRAL	DISAGREE
ALL FACULTY	**68%**	**12%**	**21%**
TYPE OF INSTITUTION			
Four Year	65	14	20
Two Year	73	6	21
CARNEGIE CLASSIFICATION			
Research	60	18	22
Doctorate	64	14	22
Comprehensive	73	11	16
Liberal Arts	56	14	29
Two Year	73	6	21
AGE			
Under 40	67	14	20
40 to 49	67	11	21
50 to 59	69	12	20
60 to 64	66	10	24
65 and over	74	13	13
GENDER			
Male	69	12	19
Female	66	10	24
DEPARTMENT			
Biological Sciences	73	11	16
Business/Communications	72	10	18
Education	43	21	37
Engineering	64	18	18
Humanities	71	11	18
Mathematics	65	13	22
Physical Sciences	75	8	17
Social Sciences	67	12	21
Other	66	10	24

Table 15

On the Whole, Undergraduates Are Now
More Willing to Work Hard in Their Studies

	AGREE	NEUTRAL	DISAGREE
ALL FACULTY	**24%**	**21%**	**55%**
TYPE OF INSTITUTION			
Four Year	27	21	52
Two Year	21	20	59
CARNEGIE CLASSIFICATION			
Research	30	25	45
Doctorate	23	24	53
Comprehensive	26	18	57
Liberal Arts	23	19	58
Two Year	21	20	59
AGE			
Under 40	13	22	65
40 to 49	21	21	58
50 to 59	32	21	48
60 to 64	31	21	48
65 and over	30	21	49
GENDER			
Male	24	23	52
Female	25	16	60
DEPARTMENT			
Biological Sciences	23	19	57
Business/Communications	26	21	52
Education	39	25	35
Engineering	33	25	42
Humanities	24	19	57
Mathematics	17	26	58
Physical Sciences	20	21	59
Social Sciences	18	20	62
Other	26	21	53

Table 16

Most Undergraduates at My Institution
Only Do Enough to Get By

	AGREE	NEUTRAL	DISAGREE
ALL FACULTY	**55%**	**12%**	**33%**
TYPE OF INSTITUTION			
Four Year	51	12	36
Two Year	63	11	27
CARNEGIE CLASSIFICATION			
Research	47	15	38
Doctorate	49	13	37
Comprehensive	57	10	32
Liberal Arts	46	9	46
Two Year	63	11	27
AGE			
Under 40	63	13	24
40 to 49	54	12	35
50 to 59	54	11	35
60 to 64	50	13	36
65 and over	57	13	30
GENDER			
Male	54	13	33
Female	56	10	34
DEPARTMENT			
Biological Sciences	54	11	35
Business/Communications	54	11	35
Education	33	21	45
Engineering	49	13	38
Humanities	62	8	30
Mathematics	55	20	25
Physical Sciences	59	10	31
Social Sciences	59	12	29
Other	50	13	37

Table 17

Grade Inflation Is a Problem at My Institution

	AGREE	NEUTRAL	DISAGREE
ALL FACULTY	**62%**	**17%**	**21%**
TYPE OF INSTITUTION			
Four Year	64	17	19
Two Year	60	16	24
CARNEGIE CLASSIFICATION			
Research	64	18	18
Doctorate	64	16	19
Comprehensive	62	18	20
Liberal Arts	65	15	20
Two Year	60	16	24
AGE			
Under 40	59	24	17
40 to 49	62	17	21
50 to 59	63	16	21
60 to 64	65	12	22
65 and over	71	11	18
GENDER			
Male	63	17	20
Female	62	16	22
DEPARTMENT			
Biological Sciences	68	12	20
Business/Communications	58	19	23
Education	57	17	26
Engineering	51	22	26
Humanities	73	12	14
Mathematics	59	16	25
Physical Sciences	60	22	18
Social Sciences	64	16	20
Other	53	21	26

Table 18

Undergraduates Today Are More Competitive Academically

	AGREE	NEUTRAL	DISAGREE
ALL FACULTY	**42%**	**27%**	**31%**
TYPE OF INSTITUTION			
Four Year	45	28	28
Two Year	36	26	38
CARNEGIE CLASSIFICATION			
Research	47	29	24
Doctorate	43	28	28
Comprehensive	44	26	31
Liberal Arts	44	28	28
Two Year	36	26	38
AGE			
Under 40	39	31	31
40 to 49	38	27	36
50 to 59	47	27	26
60 to 64	45	25	30
65 and over	46	23	30
GENDER			
Male	41	28	31
Female	43	26	31
DEPARTMENT			
Biological Sciences	34	26	39
Business/Communications	43	24	32
Education	57	28	15
Engineering	43	31	26
Humanities	46	26	28
Mathematics	26	31	43
Physical Sciences	31	33	36
Social Sciences	35	30	35
Other	48	24	28

24

Table 19

Undergraduates Have Become More Grade Conscious

	AGREE	NEUTRAL	DISAGREE
ALL FACULTY	**70%**	**18%**	**12%**
TYPE OF INSTITUTION			
Four Year	73	18	9
Two Year	63	20	17
CARNEGIE CLASSIFICATION			
Research	72	20	8
Doctorate	74	19	7
Comprehensive	73	16	11
Liberal Arts	74	17	9
Two Year	63	20	17
AGE			
Under 40	68	19	13
40 to 49	70	18	12
50 to 59	72	17	11
60 to 64	67	21	12
65 and over	67	22	11
GENDER			
Male	70	19	11
Female	68	18	14
DEPARTMENT			
Biological Sciences	65	21	14
Business/Communications	64	18	17
Education	73	18	8
Engineering	69	26	5
Humanities	77	13	9
Mathematics	67	25	9
Physical Sciences	69	21	10
Social Sciences	69	20	11
Other	66	18	16

136,194

Table 20

Today's Undergraduates Are More
Willing to Cheat in Order to Get Good Grades

	AGREE	NEUTRAL	DISAGREE
ALL FACULTY	**43%**	**40%**	**18%**
TYPE OF INSTITUTION			
Four Year	41	43	16
Two Year	45	34	21
CARNEGIE CLASSIFICATION			
Research	40	45	15
Doctorate	41	44	15
Comprehensive	43	41	16
Liberal Arts	38	41	22
Two Year	45	34	21
AGE			
Under 40	48	42	9
40 to 49	42	40	18
50 to 59	40	40	20
60 to 64	42	39	19
65 and over	47	34	19
GENDER			
Male	40	42	17
Female	48	34	18
DEPARTMENT			
Biological Sciences	34	46	20
Business/Communications	46	36	18
Education	29	43	29
Engineering	45	40	16
Humanities	44	38	18
Mathematics	40	44	16
Physical Sciences	44	44	12
Social Sciences	44	39	16
Other	44	40	17

26

Table 21

There Has Been a Widespread Lowering
of Standards in American Higher Education

	AGREE	NEUTRAL	DISAGREE
ALL FACULTY	**67%**	**15%**	**18%**
TYPE OF INSTITUTION			
Four Year	64	17	19
Two Year	73	12	16
CARNEGIE CLASSIFICATION			
Research	60	19	21
Doctorate	63	17	20
Comprehensive	67	16	18
Liberal Arts	68	14	18
Two Year	73	12	16
AGE			
Under 40	70	17	13
40 to 49	65	16	19
50 to 59	66	13	20
60 to 64	68	13	19
65 and over	73	16	11
GENDER			
Male	65	17	18
Female	72	11	17
DEPARTMENT			
Biological Sciences	71	12	17
Business/Communications	66	13	21
Education	48	20	32
Engineering	63	22	14
Humanities	72	13	15
Mathematics	63	21	16
Physical Sciences	70	15	15
Social Sciences	67	18	16
Other	65	15	20

Table 22

Academic Standards for Undergraduate
Admissions At My Institution Should Be . . .

	HIGHER	LEFT AS THEY ARE	LOWER	NOT APPLICABLE
ALL FACULTY	**57%**	**39%**	**1%**	**4%**
TYPE OF INSTITUTION				
Four Year	61	37	1	1
Two Year	49	42	0	9
CARNEGIE CLASSIFICATION				
Research	55	43	1	1
Doctorate	58	40	2	1
Comprehensive	67	30	1	1
Liberal Arts	64	34	2	0
Two Year	49	42	0	9
AGE				
Under 40	55	41	1	3
40 to 49	59	37	1	3
50 to 59	56	40	1	3
60 to 64	56	38	0	6
65 and over	59	36	2	4
GENDER				
Male	57	39	1	3
Female	57	38	1	4
DEPARTMENT				
Biological Sciences	61	34	1	4
Business/Communications	59	35	1	5
Education	51	46	1	2
Engineering	49	47	2	2
Humanities	61	35	0	3
Mathematics	62	28	2	8
Physical Sciences	62	36	0	2
Social Sciences	57	40	1	2
Other	48	46	1	4

Table 23

Academic Standards for Bachelor's Degrees at My Institution Should Be . . .

	HIGHER	LEFT AS THEY ARE	LOWER	NOT APPLICABLE
ALL FACULTY	**43%**	**31%**	**0%**	**25%**
TYPE OF INSTITUTION				
Four Year	57	41	1	1
Two Year	7	5	0	88
CARNEGIE CLASSIFICATION				
Research	53	46	1	1
Doctorate	56	42	1	1
Comprehensive	63	36	0	1
Liberal Arts	52	47	1	1
Two Year	7	5	0	88
AGE				
Under 40	47	35	0	18
40 to 49	43	28	0	28
50 to 59	41	32	1	26
60 to 64	42	32	0	26
65 and over	43	32	0	24
GENDER				
Male	45	33	0	22
Female	39	27	0	33
DEPARTMENT				
Biological Sciences	42	35	1	22
Business/Communications	43	24	1	33
Education	42	54	0	3
Engineering	41	51	0	8
Humanities	53	26	0	21
Mathematics	36	29	0	35
Physical Sciences	40	42	0	19
Social Sciences	48	30	0	22
Other	30	28	1	42

29

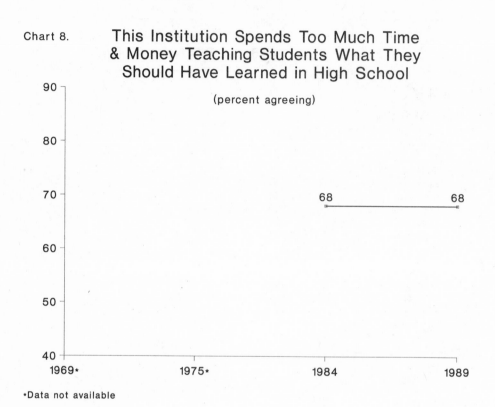

Chart 8.   **This Institution Spends Too Much Time
& Money Teaching Students What They
Should Have Learned in High School**

(percent agreeing)

90

80

70   68   68

60

50

40
1969*   1975*   1984   1989

*Data not available

30

Chart 9. **Academic Standards for Undergraduate Admissions Should Be Higher**

(percent agreeing)

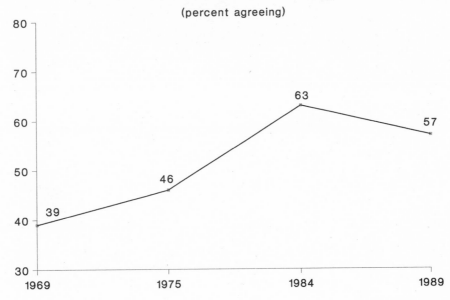

Chart 10. **Academic Standards for Bachelor's Degrees Should Be Higher**

(percent agreeing)

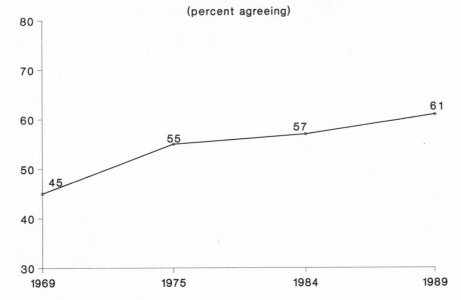

[Faculty at four-year institutions]

31

3

Attitudes About Student Life

Faculty are concerned about student life outside the classroom. Indeed, the responses of faculty to questions about the quality of student life on campuses today raise disturbing questions about the college community in its broadest sense.

We found that a third of faculty agree that there is more alcohol abuse and drug abuse among undergraduates today than five years ago. About 20 percent disagree, and 47 percent gave a neutral response to this item.

The quality of life at institutions is further diminished by crime, according to this survey. Disturbingly, 50 percent of faculty agree that there is more crime and violence on campus being committed by off-campus criminals now. While colleges should not be sealed off from the rest of the world, they should provide environments where students feel reasonably safe and secure. We should look at whether this condition is disappearing.

A majority of faculty believe that undergraduates have become more conservative in their lifestyle. An even larger number—83 percent—say that undergraduates have become more conservative politically. Such views, of course, may simply indicate the more liberal nature of the faculty.

Finally, nearly a third of the professors we surveyed note a growing trend among undergraduates to isolate themselves in small groups. It seems reasonable to suggest that students should be spending more time, not less, with different groups of peers. It is only through communal experience—which is key to the undergraduate years—that students can gain a greater understanding of diversity, and learn to celebrate it.

Table 24

Undergraduates Have Become More Conservative in Lifestyle

	AGREE	NEUTRAL	DISAGREE
ALL FACULTY	**62%**	**16%**	**23%**
TYPE OF INSTITUTION			
Four Year	63	17	20
Two Year	59	14	27
CARNEGIE CLASSIFICATION			
Research	64	19	17
Doctorate	64	16	19
Comprehensive	62	15	22
Liberal Arts	59	14	27
Two Year	59	14	27
AGE			
Under 40	62	17	21
40 to 49	64	15	20
50 to 59	60	16	24
60 to 64	59	18	24
65 and over	58	13	29
GENDER			
Male	63	17	20
Female	59	13	28
DEPARTMENT			
Biological Sciences	60	17	24
Business/Communications	58	15	27
Education	63	16	21
Engineering	49	28	23
Humanities	68	12	21
Mathematics	47	31	22
Physical Sciences	61	23	16
Social Sciences	66	13	22
Other	61	14	25

Table 25

Undergraduates Have Become More Conservative Politically

	AGREE	NEUTRAL	DISAGREE
ALL FACULTY	**83%**	**12%**	**5%**
TYPE OF INSTITUTION			
Four Year	87	9	4
Two Year	77	18	5
CARNEGIE CLASSIFICATION			
Research	86	10	4
Doctorate	86	10	4
Comprehensive	88	8	4
Liberal Arts	87	7	6
Two Year	77	18	5
AGE			
Under 40	84	12	4
40 to 49	85	11	4
50 to 59	81	13	6
60 to 64	80	16	4
65 and over	88	10	3
GENDER			
Male	85	11	4
Female	81	14	5
DEPARTMENT			
Biological Sciences	82	10	8
Business/Communications	82	12	5
Education	86	12	3
Engineering	70	23	7
Humanities	90	7	4
Mathematics	74	23	2
Physical Sciences	85	13	2
Social Sciences	94	3	2
Other	72	21	7

Table 26

There Is More Alcohol Abuse Among
Today's Undergraduates Than Five Years Ago

	AGREE	NEUTRAL	DISAGREE
ALL FACULTY	**33%**	**47%**	**20%**
TYPE OF INSTITUTION			
Four Year	31	49	19
Two Year	36	42	22
CARNEGIE CLASSIFICATION			
Research	28	53	19
Doctorate	29	48	23
Comprehensive	33	48	19
Liberal Arts	42	38	20
Two Year	36	42	22
AGE			
Under 40	32	51	17
40 to 49	33	47	20
50 to 59	33	44	23
60 to 64	31	50	19
65 and over	34	45	21
GENDER			
Male	30	49	21
Female	40	42	18
DEPARTMENT			
Biological Sciences	25	50	25
Business/Communications	28	46	26
Education	37	43	20
Engineering	24	59	17
Humanities	35	46	19
Mathematics	29	55	16
Physical Sciences	24	57	18
Social Sciences	32	47	20
Other	43	39	18

Table 27

There Is More Drug Abuse Among
Today's Undergraduates Than Five Years Ago

	AGREE	NEUTRAL	DISAGREE
ALL FACULTY	**33%**	**43%**	**25%**
TYPE OF INSTITUTION			
Four Year	30	46	24
Two Year	37	37	26
CARNEGIE CLASSIFICATION			
Research	27	50	23
Doctorate	29	45	26
Comprehensive	33	44	24
Liberal Arts	32	39	29
Two Year	37	37	26
AGE			
Under 40	27	52	21
40 to 49	35	41	24
50 to 59	34	39	27
60 to 64	30	44	26
65 and over	34	39	28
GENDER			
Male	29	44	27
Female	41	38	21
DEPARTMENT			
Biological Sciences	29	43	27
Business/Communications	30	45	25
Education	33	39	28
Engineering	30	52	18
Humanities	30	42	28
Mathematics	27	54	19
Physical Sciences	29	50	21
Social Sciences	29	42	29
Other	45	35	20

Table 28

There Is More Violence and Crime
Perpetrated by Off-Campus Criminals Now

	AGREE	NEUTRAL	DISAGREE
ALL FACULTY	**50%**	**38%**	**12%**
TYPE OF INSTITUTION			
Four Year	51	38	11
Two Year	48	38	14
CARNEGIE CLASSIFICATION			
Research	54	37	9
Doctorate	47	37	16
Comprehensive	49	41	10
Liberal Arts	51	36	13
Two Year	48	38	14
AGE			
Under 40	41	48	11
40 to 49	46	40	14
50 to 59	57	32	11
60 to 64	52	36	12
65 and over	62	31	7
GENDER			
Male	50	37	12
Female	49	40	11
DEPARTMENT			
Biological Sciences	50	38	12
Business/Communications	44	45	11
Education	53	40	7
Engineering	50	40	11
Humanities	55	31	15
Mathematics	33	56	11
Physical Sciences	57	34	9
Social Sciences	47	40	13
Other	53	36	11

Table 29

There Is a Growing Trend Among
Undergraduates to Isolate Themselves in Small Groups

	AGREE	NEUTRAL	DISAGREE
ALL FACULTY	**31%**	**53%**	**16%**
TYPE OF INSTITUTION			
Four Year	28	58	14
Two Year	37	44	19
CARNEGIE CLASSIFICATION			
Research	23	64	13
Doctorate	28	57	15
Comprehensive	30	56	14
Liberal Arts	35	46	19
Two Year	37	44	19
AGE			
Under 40	33	57	10
40 to 49	32	53	15
50 to 59	28	53	19
60 to 64	29	52	19
65 and over	34	51	15
GENDER			
Male	28	55	17
Female	37	49	14
DEPARTMENT			
Biological Sciences	24	60	16
Business/Communications	31	53	16
Education	31	51	19
Engineering	21	60	19
Humanities	33	53	13
Mathematics	26	59	15
Physical Sciences	22	64	14
Social Sciences	28	57	15
Other	39	42	19

4

Teaching, Research, and Service

One of the major issues we explored in our survey is the relationship between teaching and research. Over 70 percent of professors say that their interest is primarily in or leaning toward teaching, a heartening commitment to the education of students, although one that has declined somewhat since 1969.

Professors express this support for teaching in other ways, too. A strong majority of faculty agree that teaching effectiveness should be the primary criterion for faculty promotion. This figure, however, has been steadily declining since 1975, a worrisome trend. Yet teaching is clearly an important factor in tenure decisions: 67 percent of faculty report that student evaluations are either very important or fairly important in decisions to grant tenure.

Despite faculty support for teaching, professors are plainly experiencing increased pressure to publish. Nearly two-thirds of faculty say that they are engaged in work that they expect to lead to a publication, exhibition, or recital. Fifty-four percent agree that it is difficult to receive tenure without publishing, a rise from 41 percent since 1969. At four-year institutions, the figure is even higher.

Scholarship is of vital importance to the academic enterprise. Faculty, however, wonder if quantity is now more important than quality in published research. Over half believe that the *number* of publications is very important or fairly important in tenure decisions. Thirty-eight percent say that at their institutions publications are merely counted and not qualitatively measured.

These opinions are disturbing. Even more so is the view of over a third of the faculty that pressure to publish reduces the quality of teaching at their university. In fact, 44 percent of faculty report that the undergraduate curriculum has suffered because of faculty overspecialization.

This suggests that an appropriate balance between teaching and research has yet to be struck at many colleges. Indeed, faculty themselves recognize that the pressures may be out of hand: 68 percent agree that there need to be better ways, besides publications, to evaluate scholarly performance.

Ironically, faculty report that, just as the pressure to produce scholarly work is growing, support for it is shrinking. Only 18 percent of faculty received research support from the federal government in the past year. Even more surprising, only 41 percent received support from institution or department funds. Both these figures have dropped significantly in just five years, leaving faculty to face less support but greater demands for research.

It is reassuring to note that increased scholarly pressures have not diminished professors' commitment to the students themselves. Over 90 percent say that their relationship with undergraduates is very or fairly important to them, and 78 percent reject the idea that undergraduates should seek faculty out only during posted office hours. Moreover, 83 percent told us that they enjoy interacting informally with undergraduates outside the classroom. Obviously, in spite of their concerns about students' attitudes and behavior, faculty like their students and are committed to teaching them.

A significant minority of professors believe that fewer faculty members than in the past provide positive role models for undergraduates.

We were encouraged to find that a third of faculty reported that they provided advice, free or for a fee, to elementary or secondary schools in the past two years. In the nationwide effort to improve our schools, this is an important development. Faculty support is strong. Indeed, 82 percent of professors told us that faculty in high schools and colleges should work together to improve education in their discipline. As more and more faculty act upon this commitment, education at all levels should improve, and faculty concern about basic skills of freshmen will decline. This is an area of genuine opportunity and, hopefully, faculty will act on this commitment to cooperate with schools.

Table 30

Do Your Interests Lie Primarily in Research or in Teaching?

	PRIMARILY IN RESEARCH	LEANING TOWARD RESEARCH	LEANING TOWARD TEACHING	PRIMARILY IN TEACHING
ALL FACULTY	**6%**	**23%**	**27%**	**44%**
TYPE OF INSTITUTION				
Four Year	9	32	32	26
Two Year	1	6	16	77
CARNEGIE CLASSIFICATION				
Research	18	48	25	10
Doctorate	8	37	34	21
Comprehensive	3	20	38	39
Liberal Arts	2	14	35	49
Two Year	1	6	16	77
AGE				
Under 40	11	33	26	31
40 to 49	6	25	29	40
50 to 59	4	19	25	51
60 to 64	5	16	27	53
65 and over	9	20	20	51
GENDER				
Male	7	26	26	41
Female	4	18	28	50
DEPARTMENT				
Biological Sciences	15	29	22	33
Business/Communications	5	16	26	53
Education	3	22	34	41
Engineering	8	43	23	26
Humanities	5	24	34	37
Mathematics	3	24	13	60
Physical Sciences	9	34	24	32
Social Sciences	10	28	25	38
Other	3	14	25	59

43

Table 31

In My Undergraduate Courses, I Prefer Teaching Students
Who Have a Clear Idea of the Career They Will Be Following

	AGREE	NEUTRAL	DISAGREE
ALL FACULTY	**37%**	**32%**	**31%**
TYPE OF INSTITUTION			
Four Year	31	35	34
Two Year	50	26	24
CARNEGIE CLASSIFICATION			
Research	29	36	35
Doctorate	34	34	32
Comprehensive	32	36	32
Liberal Arts	28	28	44
Two Year	50	26	24
AGE			
Under 40	37	29	34
40 to 49	34	32	34
50 to 59	39	35	27
60 to 64	41	32	27
65 and over	45	28	27
GENDER			
Male	37	34	29
Female	38	27	35
DEPARTMENT			
Biological Sciences	28	41	32
Business/Communications	44	27	29
Education	39	44	18
Engineering	64	24	13
Humanities	26	33	40
Mathematics	33	36	31
Physical Sciences	27	45	29
Social Sciences	20	36	44
Other	63	20	17

Table 32

Teaching Effectiveness Should Be
the Primary Criterion for Promotion of Faculty

	AGREE	NEUTRAL	DISAGREE
ALL FACULTY	**62%**	**7%**	**31%**
TYPE OF INSTITUTION			
Four Year	48	9	44
Two Year	92	3	5
CARNEGIE CLASSIFICATION			
Research	22	9	69
Doctorate	41	11	48
Comprehensive	68	8	24
Liberal Arts	76	6	18
Two Year	92	3	5
AGE			
Under 40	53	9	38
40 to 49	61	7	32
50 to 59	67	6	27
60 to 64	69	6	25
65 and over	62	8	30
GENDER			
Male	58	8	34
Female	73	6	22
DEPARTMENT			
Biological Sciences	50	7	42
Business/Communications	71	5	24
Education	57	9	34
Engineering	45	9	45
Humanities	66	7	27
Mathematics	58	7	35
Physical Sciences	47	8	45
Social Sciences	50	9	41
Other	77	6	17

Table 33

How Important Are Student Evaluations of
Courses for Granting Tenure in Your Department?

	VERY IMPORTANT	FAIRLY IMPORTANT	FAIRLY UNIMPORTANT	VERY UNIMPORTANT	NO OPINION
ALL FACULTY	**26%**	**41%**	**19%**	**10%**	**4%**
TYPE OF INSTITUTION					
Four Year	25	43	21	10	2
Two Year	29	36	15	10	9
CARNEGIE CLASSIFICATION					
Research	10	41	30	16	2
Doctorate	19	42	26	11	1
Comprehensive	37	44	13	4	2
Liberal Arts	44	45	6	2	3
Two Year	29	36	15	10	9
AGE					
Under 40	26	35	22	12	5
40 to 49	27	43	18	9	4
50 to 59	28	39	19	9	4
60 to 64	23	46	19	10	2
65 and over	16	43	22	12	7
GENDER					
Male	24	42	20	9	4
Female	32	37	16	10	4
DEPARTMENT					
Biological Sciences	19	44	20	15	2
Business/Communications	28	37	17	11	7
Education	33	43	15	7	3
Engineering	18	38	31	10	4
Humanities	26	40	21	9	4
Mathematics	27	44	13	11	5
Physical Sciences	21	48	21	8	2
Social Sciences	26	40	20	12	1
Other	31	39	16	7	7

Table 34

Are You Currently Engaged in Any Scholarly Work That You Expect to Lead to a Publication, an Exhibit, or a Musical Recital?

	YES	NO
ALL FACULTY	**66%**	**34%**
TYPE OF INSTITUTION		
Four Year	83	17
Two Year	32	68
CARNEGIE CLASSIFICATION		
Research	95	5
Doctorate	88	12
Comprehensive	75	25
Liberal Arts	68	32
Two Year	32	68
AGE		
Under 40	78	22
40 to 49	69	31
50 to 59	61	39
60 to 64	54	46
65 and over	56	44
GENDER		
Male	69	31
Female	60	40
DEPARTMENT		
Biological Sciences	78	22
Business/Communications	59	41
Education	77	23
Engineering	80	20
Humanities	73	27
Mathematics	58	42
Physical Sciences	75	25
Social Sciences	71	29
Other	45	55

Table 35

In My Department It Is Difficult for a Person
to Achieve Tenure If He or She Does Not Publish

	AGREE	NEUTRAL	DISAGREE
ALL FACULTY	**54%**	**9%**	**37%**
TYPE OF INSTITUTION			
Four Year	77	4	18
Two Year	6	19	75
CARNEGIE CLASSIFICATION			
Research	94	1	5
Doctorate	89	2	9
Comprehensive	65	7	28
Liberal Arts	39	10	51
Two Year	6	19	75
AGE			
Under 40	65	8	27
40 to 49	54	8	37
50 to 59	49	10	41
60 to 64	46	12	43
65 and over	48	12	40
GENDER			
Male	57	9	33
Female	45	9	46
DEPARTMENT			
Biological Sciences	64	5	31
Business/Communications	50	10	40
Education	75	4	21
Engineering	81	7	12
Humanities	49	10	41
Mathematics	48	6	46
Physical Sciences	64	11	25
Social Sciences	60	6	34
Other	39	14	47

Table 36

How Important Is the Number of
Publications for Granting Tenure in Your Department?

	VERY IMPORTANT	FAIRLY IMPORTANT	FAIRLY UNIMPORTANT	VERY UNIMPORTANT	NO OPINION
ALL FACULTY	**28%**	**29%**	**14%**	**22%**	**7%**
TYPE OF INSTITUTION					
Four Year	41	39	11	7	2
Two Year	2	8	19	54	17
CARNEGIE CLASSIFICATION					
Research	56	38	4	1	1
Doctorate	54	36	7	2	1
Comprehensive	29	42	16	10	3
Liberal Arts	8	32	31	23	6
Two Year	2	8	19	54	17
AGE					
Under 40	38	29	11	16	7
40 to 49	28	30	14	22	6
50 to 59	24	28	15	26	7
60 to 64	25	26	14	28	7
65 and over	21	30	20	19	10
GENDER					
Male	29	31	13	20	6
Female	25	23	15	27	9
DEPARTMENT					
Biological Sciences	38	27	13	19	4
Business/Communications	31	21	13	27	9
Education	44	36	6	10	4
Engineering	44	38	10	5	3
Humanities	23	34	15	22	6
Mathematics	16	31	15	29	9
Physical Sciences	31	33	18	14	4
Social Sciences	35	29	12	23	1
Other	19	22	16	29	14

Table 37

At My Institution Publications Used for Tenure and Promotion Are Just Counted, Not Qualitatively Measured

	AGREE	NEUTRAL	DISAGREE
ALL FACULTY	**38%**	**25%**	**37%**
TYPE OF INSTITUTION			
Four Year	47	13	40
Two Year	19	50	31
CARNEGIE CLASSIFICATION			
Research	42	9	49
Doctorate	52	10	38
Comprehensive	54	15	32
Liberal Arts	33	28	39
Two Year	19	50	31
AGE			
Under 40	41	28	31
40 to 49	39	22	38
50 to 59	36	26	38
60 to 64	33	29	38
65 and over	39	23	38
GENDER			
Male	38	25	37
Female	38	26	36
DEPARTMENT			
Biological Sciences	48	22	30
Business/Communications	43	25	33
Education	51	11	38
Engineering	51	14	36
Humanities	36	25	39
Mathematics	31	40	30
Physical Sciences	33	23	44
Social Sciences	38	20	42
Other	31	35	34

Table 38

The Pressure to Publish Reduces
the Quality of Teaching at My University

	AGREE	NEUTRAL	DISAGREE
ALL FACULTY	**35%**	**19%**	**46%**
TYPE OF INSTITUTION			
Four Year	45	12	43
Two Year	14	34	52
CARNEGIE CLASSIFICATION			
Research	52	10	38
Doctorate	53	12	35
Comprehensive	41	13	46
Liberal Arts	22	17	61
Two Year	14	34	52
AGE			
Under 40	43	20	37
40 to 49	34	18	48
50 to 59	32	18	50
60 to 64	31	25	45
65 and over	39	21	40
GENDER			
Male	36	19	45
Female	34	19	47
DEPARTMENT			
Biological Sciences	40	13	47
Business/Communications	37	22	42
Education	48	12	40
Engineering	53	13	34
Humanities	31	19	50
Mathematics	22	29	49
Physical Sciences	37	19	45
Social Sciences	35	15	50
Other	31	25	44

Table 39

At My Institution We Need Better Ways, Besides Publications, to Evaluate the Scholarly Performance of the Faculty

	AGREE	NEUTRAL	DISAGREE
ALL FACULTY	**68%**	**19%**	**13%**
TYPE OF INSTITUTION			
Four Year	74	12	14
Two Year	55	33	12
CARNEGIE CLASSIFICATION			
Research	69	12	19
Doctorate	77	10	14
Comprehensive	79	12	9
Liberal Arts	69	16	15
Two Year	55	33	12
AGE			
Under 40	68	17	15
40 to 49	67	19	14
50 to 59	66	20	13
60 to 64	70	22	8
65 and over	76	13	10
GENDER			
Male	68	19	14
Female	68	20	12
DEPARTMENT			
Biological Sciences	62	21	17
Business/Communications	68	21	11
Education	83	7	10
Engineering	80	12	8
Humanities	67	18	15
Mathematics	57	27	16
Physical Sciences	66	20	14
Social Sciences	62	20	18
Other	72	20	8

Table 40

The Undergraduate Curriculum Has Suffered from the Specialization of Faculty Members

	AGREE	NEUTRAL	DISAGREE
ALL FACULTY	**44%**	**22%**	**35%**
TYPE OF INSTITUTION			
Four Year	46	19	35
Two Year	40	27	33
CARNEGIE CLASSIFICATION			
Research	43	20	37
Doctorate	44	20	36
Comprehensive	47	18	35
Liberal Arts	52	19	30
Two Year	40	27	33
AGE			
Under 40	39	21	40
40 to 49	46	20	34
50 to 59	44	24	33
60 to 64	45	25	31
65 and over	42	23	35
GENDER			
Male	45	21	33
Female	40	22	38
DEPARTMENT			
Biological Sciences	47	15	38
Business/Communications	43	19	38
Education	48	21	31
Engineering	34	23	43
Humanities	50	21	29
Mathematics	30	30	40
Physical Sciences	42	21	38
Social Sciences	50	21	29
Other	35	26	39

Table 41

How Important to You Is Your Relationship with Undergraduates?

	VERY IMPORTANT	FAIRLY IMPORTANT	FAIRLY UNIMPORTANT	NOT AT ALL IMPORTANT
ALL FACULTY	**57%**	**35%**	**6%**	**2%**
TYPE OF INSTITUTION				
Four Year	51	38	8	2
Two Year	68	30	2	0
CARNEGIE CLASSIFICATION				
Research	36	45	14	4
Doctorate	49	40	8	3
Comprehensive	60	34	5	1
Liberal Arts	72	26	2	0
Two Year	68	30	2	0
AGE				
Under 40	51	40	7	2
40 to 49	54	38	6	2
50 to 59	60	33	5	2
60 to 64	62	31	6	1
65 and over	60	30	8	2
GENDER				
Male	54	37	7	2
Female	62	31	5	1
DEPARTMENT				
Biological Sciences	60	32	8	0
Business/Communications	59	34	6	1
Education	48	30	10	12
Engineering	50	43	7	0
Humanities	61	34	5	0
Mathematics	52	41	7	0
Physical Sciences	46	45	8	1
Social Sciences	49	41	8	2
Other	65	30	4	2

Table 42

Undergraduates Should Seek Out
Faculty Only During Posted Office Hours

	AGREE	NEUTRAL	DISAGREE
ALL FACULTY	**15%**	**7%**	**78%**
TYPE OF INSTITUTION			
Four Year	14	8	78
Two Year	16	5	78
CARNEGIE CLASSIFICATION			
Research	15	10	74
Doctorate	15	8	77
Comprehensive	13	7	80
Liberal Arts	12	4	84
Two Year	16	5	78
AGE			
Under 40	17	8	75
40 to 49	15	7	78
50 to 59	14	6	80
60 to 64	13	8	79
65 and over	15	5	80
GENDER			
Male	13	7	79
Female	19	6	75
DEPARTMENT			
Biological Sciences	11	7	82
Business/Communications	16	9	76
Education	11	13	76
Engineering	23	12	66
Humanities	15	5	80
Mathematics	12	8	80
Physical Sciences	8	7	85
Social Sciences	17	7	76
Other	16	6	78

Table 43

I Enjoy Interacting Informally
with Undergraduates Outside the Classroom

	AGREE	NEUTRAL	DISAGREE
ALL FACULTY	**83%**	**10%**	**7%**
TYPE OF INSTITUTION			
Four Year	83	11	7
Two Year	84	8	8
CARNEGIE CLASSIFICATION			
Research	77	15	8
Doctorate	83	10	7
Comprehensive	85	9	6
Liberal Arts	92	5	4
Two Year	84	8	8
AGE			
Under 40	84	8	8
40 to 49	83	10	8
50 to 59	83	12	5
60 to 64	84	9	7
65 and over	80	9	11
GENDER			
Male	84	10	7
Female	81	10	9
DEPARTMENT			
Biological Sciences	87	9	4
Business/Communications	81	9	10
Education	75	21	4
Engineering	83	9	9
Humanities	84	8	8
Mathematics	87	11	2
Physical Sciences	84	12	5
Social Sciences	86	8	6
Other	81	10	9

56

Table 44

Fewer Faculty Members Provide Positive
Role Models to Our Undergraduates Than in the Past

	AGREE	NEUTRAL	DISAGREE
ALL FACULTY	**39%**	**26%**	**35%**
TYPE OF INSTITUTION			
Four Year	39	28	33
Two Year	40	21	39
CARNEGIE CLASSIFICATION			
Research	39	33	29
Doctorate	41	27	32
Comprehensive	39	25	36
Liberal Arts	33	26	41
Two Year	40	21	39
AGE			
Under 40	36	33	31
40 to 49	38	26	36
50 to 59	40	23	38
60 to 64	40	25	35
65 and over	51	21	28
GENDER			
Male	41	27	32
Female	35	22	42
DEPARTMENT			
Biological Sciences	39	28	33
Business/Communications	42	20	38
Education	36	25	40
Engineering	47	37	17
Humanities	34	29	37
Mathematics	38	33	29
Physical Sciences	37	31	31
Social Sciences	35	31	34
Other	47	15	38

Table 45

During the Past 12 Months, Did You
Receive Research Support from Federal Agencies?

	YES	NO
ALL FACULTY	**18%**	**82%**
TYPE OF INSTITUTION		
Four Year	24	76
Two Year	5	95
CARNEGIE CLASSIFICATION		
Research	43	57
Doctorate	18	82
Comprehensive	10	90
Liberal Arts	11	89
Two Year	5	95
AGE		
Under 40	24	76
40 to 49	19	81
50 to 59	15	85
60 to 64	11	89
65 and over	11	89
GENDER		
Male	19	81
Female	14	86
DEPARTMENT		
Biological Sciences	41	59
Business/Communications	9	91
Education	18	82
Engineering	47	53
Humanities	8	92
Mathematics	22	78
Physical Sciences	44	56
Social Sciences	16	84
Other	10	90

Table 46

During the Past 12 Months, Did You Receive Research Support from Institutional or Departmental Funds?

	YES	NO
ALL FACULTY	**41%**	**59%**
TYPE OF INSTITUTION		
Four Year	51	49
Two Year	23	77
CARNEGIE CLASSIFICATION		
Research	59	41
Doctorate	55	45
Comprehensive	43	57
Liberal Arts	44	56
Two Year	23	77
AGE		
Under 40	55	45
40 to 49	44	56
50 to 59	36	64
60 to 64	27	73
65 and over	29	71
GENDER		
Male	42	58
Female	40	60
DEPARTMENT		
Biological Sciences	59	41
Business/Communications	36	64
Education	42	58
Engineering	49	51
Humanities	41	59
Mathematics	26	74
Physical Sciences	51	49
Social Sciences	47	53
Other	36	64

Table 47

During the Past Two Years, Have You Served as a Paid
or Unpaid Consultant to a Private Business or Industry?

	YES, PAID	YES, UNPAID	NO
ALL FACULTY	**30%**	**9%**	**62%**
TYPE OF INSTITUTION			
Four Year	32	8	60
Two Year	25	11	64
CARNEGIE CLASSIFICATION			
Research	35	6	59
Doctorate	35	7	58
Comprehensive	31	10	59
Liberal Arts	20	7	74
Two Year	25	11	64
AGE			
Under 40	27	10	63
40 to 49	33	9	58
50 to 59	31	8	60
60 to 64	21	6	73
65 and over	17	13	70
GENDER			
Male	33	8	59
Female	22	10	68
DEPARTMENT			
Biological Sciences	27	9	64
Business/Communications	41	13	46
Education	20	8	71
Engineering	58	5	37
Humanities	22	7	71
Mathematics	24	3	73
Physical Sciences	34	7	59
Social Sciences	28	4	68
Other	27	15	58

Table 48

During the Past Two Years, Have You Served as a Paid or Unpaid Consultant to Schools (Elementary or Secondary)?

	YES, PAID	YES, UNPAID	NO
ALL FACULTY	**10%**	**23%**	**67%**
TYPE OF INSTITUTION			
Four Year	12	22	67
Two Year	7	25	69
CARNEGIE CLASSIFICATION			
Research	9	18	73
Doctorate	13	20	67
Comprehensive	14	24	62
Liberal Arts	8	28	64
Two Year	7	25	69
AGE			
Under 40	8	23	70
40 to 49	12	24	64
50 to 59	10	25	66
60 to 64	8	13	79
65 and over	7	18	75
GENDER			
Male	10	21	69
Female	10	27	63
DEPARTMENT			
Biological Sciences	4	31	65
Business/Communications	6	21	73
Education	47	33	21
Engineering	2	13	85
Humanities	11	24	64
Mathematics	5	15	80
Physical Sciences	6	17	77
Social Sciences	8	15	76
Other	8	27	65

Table 49

Faculty Members in High Schools and Colleges Should
Work Together to Improve Education in My Discipline

	AGREE	NEUTRAL	DISAGREE
ALL FACULTY	**82%**	**12%**	**6%**
TYPE OF INSTITUTION			
Four Year	79	14	7
Two Year	89	8	3
CARNEGIE CLASSIFICATION			
Research	72	18	10
Doctorate	78	14	8
Comprehensive	84	11	5
Liberal Arts	85	10	5
Two Year	89	8	3
AGE			
Under 40	79	14	7
40 to 49	83	12	5
50 to 59	83	11	6
60 to 64	85	11	5
65 and over	79	15	5
GENDER			
Male	82	12	6
Female	83	11	6
DEPARTMENT			
Biological Sciences	88	10	2
Business/Communications	70	20	10
Education	90	7	3
Engineering	73	19	8
Humanities	87	8	5
Mathematics	92	5	3
Physical Sciences	92	4	3
Social Sciences	74	17	9
Other	83	12	5

62

Chart 11.

My Interests Lie Primarily in
or Leaning Toward Teaching

(percent agreeing)

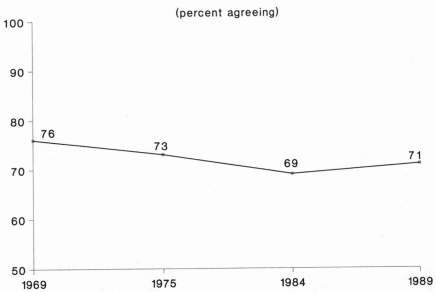

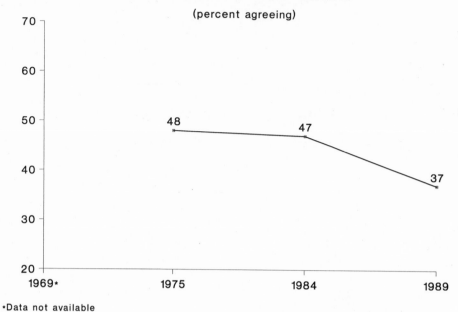

Chart 12.

Prefer Teaching Students with a Clear Idea of Their Career

(percent agreeing)

*Data not available

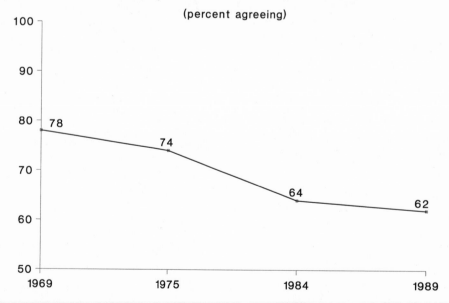

Chart 13.

Teaching Effectiveness Should Be the Primary Criterion for Promotion

(percent agreeing)

64

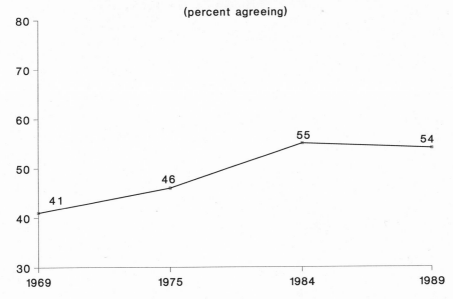

Chart 14. **It Is Difficult for a Person to Receive Tenure If He/She Does Not Publish**

(percent agreeing)

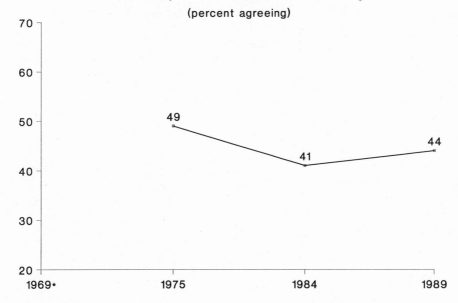

Chart 15. **Undergraduate Curriculum Has Suffered from Specialization of Faculty**

(percent agreeing)

*Data not available

65

Chart 16. **Undergraduates Should Seek Out Faculty Only During Posted Office Hours**

(percent disagreeing)

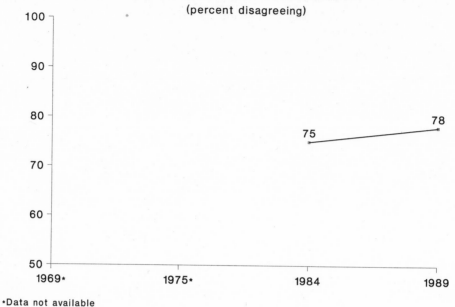

*Data not available

Chart 17. **Received Research Support in Last 12 Months from Federal Agencies**

(percent responding "Yes")

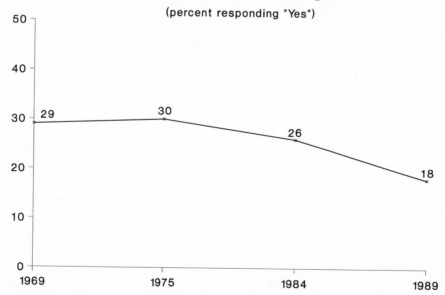

66

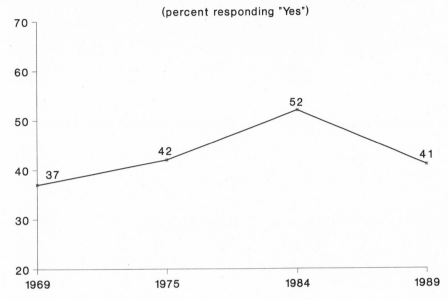

Chart 18.   **Received Research Support in Last
12 Months from Institutional Funds**

(percent responding "Yes")

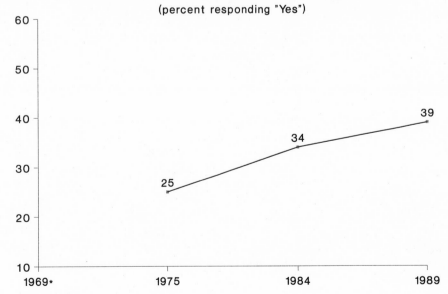

Chart 19.   **Served as a Consultant to Private
Business or Industry in Last Two Years**

(percent responding "Yes")

*Data not available

67

5

Status of the Profession

An important element of academic quality is the faculty's feelings about their profession. We examined these attitudes within the professoriate today in terms of excitement about their field of study and agreement with colleagues about the standards of good scholarship; of job prospects for young faculty members; of general enthusiasm about their career; of stress; and of financial support in salaries and in funding for scholarship.

Faculty responses were fairly upbeat. Although financial support for research appears to have become harder to obtain, 56 percent find a general agreement about what constitutes good scholarship, and 77 percent say that exciting things are happening in their fields.

When asked if this was a "poor time for any young person to begin an academic career," 66 percent of our respondents disagreed, with about half indicating that job prospects for undergraduates in their fields are better than they were five years ago. In spite of the fact that 44 percent of responding professors find their work a source of considerable strain in their lives, they do not regret having chosen that path. A significant 74 percent disagreed with the statement: "I often wish I had entered another profession."

These responses, combined with the strong importance faculty attach to their academic discipline, which we report in Chapter 6, reveal an overall positive attitude about the profession itself.

Our findings regarding financial issues are less encouraging. Although faculty salary ratings have begun to recover from their 1984 low, there is general agreement, at all types of institutions, that salaries have not kept up with the rate of inflation. Further, considering the importance of research, which often requires supplemental support, it's significant that, according to the faculty, research funds are increasingly difficult to obtain. Again, this is true at all types of institutions.

Also, we were struck by the pressure faculty feel about their professional activity. Forty-four percent told us that their work "is the source of considerable personal strain," and nearly the same number say they hardly ever get time to give a piece of work the attention it deserves. The age of the respondent is significant on questions about stress, with younger faculty feeling more pressure than older colleagues. Among the disciplines, engineering faculty report more stress than their colleagues in other fields.

The feelings of much of the professoriate might be summed up by these remarks from a professor at a Research university:

> You have to be a workaholic to do this job, but I personally can't imagine another setting that has such high intellectual expectations *and* provides such autonomy as this occupation. It is not always a joy, but it represents the best job for me. I'm in for the duration.

Another professor expressed similar sentiments when he told us:

> For all of the dissatisfaction I have registered in the preceding pages, I regard my career as a teacher and scholar as a great privilege, which I would not give up for any amount of money. After 19 years, I enjoy teaching more than ever and become restless if on leave.

Table 50

Exciting Developments Are Now Taking Place in My Discipline

	AGREE	NEUTRAL	DISAGREE
ALL FACULTY	**77%**	**12%**	**12%**
TYPE OF INSTITUTION			
Four Year	77	12	11
Two Year	76	11	13
CARNEGIE CLASSIFICATION			
Research	77	11	11
Doctorate	78	13	9
Comprehensive	77	12	11
Liberal Arts	76	14	10
Two Year	76	11	13
AGE			
Under 40	81	10	9
40 to 49	79	11	10
50 to 59	75	11	13
60 to 64	67	17	16
65 and over	76	13	11
GENDER			
Male	76	12	11
Female	78	10	12
DEPARTMENT			
Biological Sciences	94	3	3
Business/Communications	75	15	10
Education	82	9	9
Engineering	84	10	6
Humanities	68	14	19
Mathematics	77	15	7
Physical Sciences	94	3	2
Social Sciences	66	16	18
Other	82	9	9

Table 51

In My Discipline, Most Faculty
Agree on the Standards of Good Scholarship

	AGREE	NEUTRAL	DISAGREE
ALL FACULTY	**56%**	**12%**	**32%**
TYPE OF INSTITUTION			
Four Year	55	11	34
Two Year	59	14	28
CARNEGIE CLASSIFICATION			
Research	54	10	36
Doctorate	53	11	37
Comprehensive	56	12	32
Liberal Arts	61	10	29
Two Year	59	14	28
AGE			
Under 40	48	13	39
40 to 49	55	11	34
50 to 59	60	12	28
60 to 64	62	11	27
65 and over	62	11	27
GENDER			
Male	56	12	31
Female	56	10	34
DEPARTMENT			
Biological Sciences	66	12	22
Business/Communications	45	15	40
Education	39	11	50
Engineering	55	21	24
Humanities	59	9	32
Mathematics	64	19	18
Physical Sciences	77	11	13
Social Sciences	53	10	37
Other	56	11	33

Table 52

This Is a Poor Time for Any Young Person
to Begin an Academic Career

	AGREE	NEUTRAL	DISAGREE
ALL FACULTY	**20%**	**14%**	**66%**
TYPE OF INSTITUTION			
Four Year	21	15	64
Two Year	18	11	71
CARNEGIE CLASSIFICATION			
Research	22	16	62
Doctorate	22	15	63
Comprehensive	20	16	64
Liberal Arts	17	13	71
Two Year	18	11	71
AGE			
Under 40	21	16	63
40 to 49	19	13	67
50 to 59	20	14	67
60 to 64	22	14	65
65 and over	17	10	74
GENDER			
Male	20	15	65
Female	19	12	69
DEPARTMENT			
Biological Sciences	19	12	69
Business/Communications	19	15	66
Education	12	11	77
Engineering	30	15	55
Humanities	24	15	62
Mathematics	16	15	69
Physical Sciences	18	16	66
Social Sciences	19	14	67
Other	18	11	71

Table 53

How Have Job Prospects for Undergraduates in Your Field Changed over the Past Five Years?

	WAS NOT TEACHING	BETTER	ABOUT THE SAME	WORSE
ALL FACULTY	8%	49%	31%	12%
TYPE OF INSTITUTION				
Four Year	9	47	33	11
Two Year	5	52	28	15
CARNEGIE CLASSIFICATION				
Research	9	43	36	11
Doctorate	9	48	33	11
Comprehensive	8	52	30	10
Liberal Arts	12	45	32	11
Two Year	5	52	28	15
AGE				
Under 40	27	39	24	10
40 to 49	6	52	32	10
50 to 59	1	50	35	13
60 to 64	3	48	32	17
65 and over	2	56	29	14
GENDER				
Male	7	48	33	12
Female	10	51	27	12
DEPARTMENT				
Biological Sciences	7	49	29	15
Business/Communications	9	52	29	10
Education	14	53	26	7
Engineering	12	49	33	6
Humanities	6	41	37	15
Mathematics	7	69	20	4
Physical Sciences	9	46	30	15
Social Sciences	6	40	40	13
Other	7	59	22	12

74

Table 54

If I Had It to Do Over Again,
I Would Not Become a College Teacher

	AGREE	NEUTRAL	DISAGREE
ALL FACULTY	**15%**	**9%**	**77%**
TYPE OF INSTITUTION			
Four Year	16	9	75
Two Year	13	8	79
CARNEGIE CLASSIFICATION			
Research	14	11	75
Doctorate	16	10	74
Comprehensive	17	7	75
Liberal Arts	14	8	78
Two Year	13	8	79
AGE			
Under 40	15	10	76
40 to 49	17	8	75
50 to 59	13	8	79
60 to 64	13	11	77
65 and over	12	10	78
GENDER			
Male	15	9	76
Female	14	7	79
DEPARTMENT			
Biological Sciences	15	8	77
Business/Communications	12	9	79
Education	15	10	76
Engineering	15	11	74
Humanities	17	7	76
Mathematics	16	6	78
Physical Sciences	14	11	74
Social Sciences	15	8	76
Other	13	10	77

Table 55

I Am More Enthusiastic About My Work
Now Than When I Began My Academic Career

	AGREE	NEUTRAL	DISAGREE
ALL FACULTY	**44%**	**22%**	**34%**
TYPE OF INSTITUTION			
Four Year	43	24	33
Two Year	47	18	35
CARNEGIE CLASSIFICATION			
Research	41	26	33
Doctorate	39	25	36
Comprehensive	45	22	33
Liberal Arts	47	23	30
Two Year	47	18	35
AGE			
Under 40	46	24	29
40 to 49	46	22	32
50 to 59	41	22	37
60 to 64	42	22	36
65 and over	46	19	35
GENDER			
Male	42	24	34
Female	49	18	33
DEPARTMENT			
Biological Sciences	37	26	36
Business/Communications	45	22	32
Education	45	22	32
Engineering	40	27	33
Humanities	45	20	35
Mathematics	49	24	27
Physical Sciences	35	29	36
Social Sciences	44	22	34
Other	48	19	33

76

Table 56

I Often Wish I Had Entered Another Profession

	AGREE	NEUTRAL	DISAGREE
ALL FACULTY	**17%**	**8%**	**74%**
TYPE OF INSTITUTION			
Four Year	17	9	74
Two Year	19	6	75
CARNEGIE CLASSIFICATION			
Research	14	10	77
Doctorate	19	8	73
Comprehensive	20	9	71
Liberal Arts	15	9	77
Two Year	19	6	75
AGE			
Under 40	18	12	70
40 to 49	18	8	74
50 to 59	17	7	76
60 to 64	17	9	75
65 and over	15	8	78
GENDER			
Male	17	9	75
Female	19	7	74
DEPARTMENT			
Biological Sciences	14	9	77
Business/Communications	13	10	78
Education	11	10	79
Engineering	17	12	71
Humanities	19	7	74
Mathematics	15	6	79
Physical Sciences	15	8	77
Social Sciences	17	7	76
Other	23	9	68

Table 57

During the Past Two Years, Have You
Ever Considered a Permanent Departure From Academia?

	I HAVE GIVEN IT SERIOUS CONSIDERATION	I HAVE CONSIDERED IT, BUT NOT SERIOUSLY	NO
ALL FACULTY	**24%**	**31%**	**45%**
TYPE OF INSTITUTION			
Four Year	24	33	43
Two Year	24	26	50
CARNEGIE CLASSIFICATION			
Research	21	32	47
Doctorate	26	31	43
Comprehensive	25	35	40
Liberal Arts	26	33	41
Two Year	24	26	50
AGE			
Under 40	32	34	34
40 to 49	23	33	43
50 to 59	20	32	49
60 to 64	25	22	53
65 and over	16	20	64
GENDER			
Male	23	31	47
Female	27	31	42
DEPARTMENT			
Biological Sciences	21	35	44
Business/Communications	29	25	46
Education	25	28	47
Engineering	19	42	39
Humanities	23	30	47
Mathematics	16	28	56
Physical Sciences	20	33	47
Social Sciences	21	33	46
Other	29	31	40

Table 58

I Feel Trapped in a Profession
with Limited Opportunities for Advancement

	AGREE	NEUTRAL	DISAGREE
ALL FACULTY	**20%**	**10%**	**70%**
TYPE OF INSTITUTION			
Four Year	19	11	71
Two Year	22	9	70
CARNEGIE CLASSIFICATION			
Research	14	10	75
Doctorate	20	11	70
Comprehensive	22	11	66
Liberal Arts	18	10	73
Two Year	22	9	70
AGE			
Under 40	23	13	64
40 to 49	22	9	69
50 to 59	17	10	73
60 to 64	15	12	73
65 and over	16	9	75
GENDER			
Male	19	11	70
Female	21	8	71
DEPARTMENT			
Biological Sciences	19	14	67
Business/Communications	18	9	74
Education	15	10	74
Engineering	17	12	70
Humanities	23	9	68
Mathematics	17	10	73
Physical Sciences	15	10	75
Social Sciences	19	8	73
Other	22	11	67

Table 59

I Tend to Subordinate All
Aspects of My Life to My Work

	AGREE	NEUTRAL	DISAGREE
ALL FACULTY	**40%**	**9%**	**50%**
TYPE OF INSTITUTION			
Four Year	45	10	46
Two Year	32	8	59
CARNEGIE CLASSIFICATION			
Research	46	10	44
Doctorate	42	9	49
Comprehensive	44	10	46
Liberal Arts	47	10	43
Two Year	32	8	59
AGE			
Under 40	46	9	45
40 to 49	40	8	52
50 to 59	38	9	53
60 to 64	40	14	47
65 and over	40	13	47
GENDER			
Male	39	10	50
Female	43	7	50
DEPARTMENT			
Biological Sciences	44	10	46
Business/Communications	41	8	50
Education	41	8	50
Engineering	53	11	36
Humanities	45	9	46
Mathematics	32	15	53
Physical Sciences	37	8	55
Social Sciences	35	9	57
Other	36	9	55

Table 60

I Hardly Ever Get Time to Give a
Piece of Work the Attention It Deserves

	AGREE	NEUTRAL	DISAGREE
ALL FACULTY	**43%**	**13%**	**44%**
TYPE OF INSTITUTION			
Four Year	47	13	40
Two Year	36	13	51
CARNEGIE CLASSIFICATION			
Research	45	12	42
Doctorate	45	15	40
Comprehensive	50	13	37
Liberal Arts	46	11	42
Two Year	36	13	51
AGE			
Under 40	53	13	34
40 to 49	49	13	39
50 to 59	38	14	48
60 to 64	33	14	53
65 and over	29	11	60
GENDER			
Male	42	15	44
Female	47	9	43
DEPARTMENT			
Biological Sciences	46	11	43
Business/Communications	43	15	42
Education	47	11	42
Engineering	52	15	33
Humanities	47	11	43
Mathematics	36	13	51
Physical Sciences	42	17	41
Social Sciences	40	17	43
Other	40	11	49

Table 61

My Job Is the Source of Considerable Personal Strain

	AGREE	NEUTRAL	DISAGREE
ALL FACULTY	**44%**	**11%**	**45%**
TYPE OF INSTITUTION			
Four Year	46	11	42
Two Year	38	10	52
CARNEGIE CLASSIFICATION			
Research	48	12	41
Doctorate	46	12	41
Comprehensive	45	11	44
Liberal Arts	48	11	42
Two Year	38	10	52
AGE			
Under 40	53	13	34
40 to 49	44	11	45
50 to 59	41	9	50
60 to 64	41	12	47
65 and over	26	9	64
GENDER			
Male	40	12	47
Female	51	8	41
DEPARTMENT			
Biological Sciences	47	9	45
Business/Communications	39	13	48
Education	42	7	51
Engineering	50	19	31
Humanities	48	10	42
Mathematics	35	9	56
Physical Sciences	36	11	53
Social Sciences	39	11	50
Other	48	12	40

Table 62

How Would You Rate Your Own Salary?

	EXCELLENT	GOOD	FAIR	POOR
ALL FACULTY	**9%**	**39%**	**31%**	**21%**
TYPE OF INSTITUTION				
Four Year	7	33	35	25
Two Year	13	49	24	14
CARNEGIE CLASSIFICATION				
Research	9	36	34	22
Doctorate	6	32	37	26
Comprehensive	6	34	36	24
Liberal Arts	4	25	33	38
Two Year	13	49	24	14
AGE				
Under 40	5	30	38	28
40 to 49	7	39	29	26
50 to 59	11	42	32	16
60 to 64	14	42	30	14
65 and over	15	41	29	15
GENDER				
Male	9	39	32	20
Female	8	37	29	25
DEPARTMENT				
Biological Sciences	9	40	33	17
Business/Communications	9	42	30	19
Education	4	34	37	24
Engineering	12	33	36	19
Humanities	6	37	33	23
Mathematics	10	41	27	22
Physical Sciences	7	42	30	20
Social Sciences	8	37	31	24
Other	13	39	28	20

Table 63

On the Whole, Faculty Salaries Here
Have Kept Up with the Rate of Inflation

	AGREE	NEUTRAL	DISAGREE
ALL FACULTY	**25%**	**8%**	**67%**
TYPE OF INSTITUTION			
Four Year	22	8	69
Two Year	31	7	61
CARNEGIE CLASSIFICATION			
Research	24	9	67
Doctorate	21	9	71
Comprehensive	21	8	71
Liberal Arts	23	7	70
Two Year	31	7	61
AGE			
Under 40	22	9	69
40 to 49	25	9	66
50 to 59	26	7	67
60 to 64	28	8	64
65 and over	31	6	63
GENDER			
Male	27	8	65
Female	22	8	70
DEPARTMENT			
Biological Sciences	28	10	63
Business/Communications	22	8	70
Education	19	5	77
Engineering	30	16	53
Humanities	26	8	66
Mathematics	27	10	63
Physical Sciences	26	14	60
Social Sciences	24	6	70
Other	28	6	66

Table 64

During the Past Two or Three Years, Financial Support for Work in My Discipline Has Become Harder to Obtain

	AGREE	NEUTRAL	DISAGREE
ALL FACULTY	**54%**	**32%**	**15%**
TYPE OF INSTITUTION			
Four Year	58	27	15
Two Year	46	41	13
CARNEGIE CLASSIFICATION			
Research	63	21	16
Doctorate	59	25	15
Comprehensive	53	31	16
Liberal Arts	53	35	13
Two Year	46	41	13
AGE			
Under 40	54	32	13
40 to 49	53	32	15
50 to 59	51	33	16
60 to 64	55	36	9
65 and over	62	19	19
GENDER			
Male	53	32	15
Female	55	30	15
DEPARTMENT			
Biological Sciences	63	25	12
Business/Communications	38	41	21
Education	66	20	14
Engineering	52	34	14
Humanities	53	33	13
Mathematics	43	44	13
Physical Sciences	65	25	10
Social Sciences	54	33	13
Other	58	26	16

Table 65

I Would Exercise an Early
Retirement Option If It Were Offered to Me

	AGREE	NEUTRAL	DISAGREE
ALL FACULTY	**44%**	**16%**	**40%**
TYPE OF INSTITUTION			
Four Year	42	17	41
Two Year	50	13	38
CARNEGIE CLASSIFICATION			
Research	37	21	43
Doctorate	42	17	41
Comprehensive	47	14	38
Liberal Arts	38	19	43
Two Year	50	13	38
AGE			
Under 40	40	28	33
40 to 49	47	16	37
50 to 59	48	13	39
60 to 64	43	9	48
65 and over	23	9	68
GENDER			
Male	44	16	40
Female	46	16	39
DEPARTMENT			
Biological Sciences	46	17	37
Business/Communications	41	20	39
Education	51	12	36
Engineering	38	21	41
Humanities	45	15	40
Mathematics	36	17	47
Physical Sciences	31	19	50
Social Sciences	42	14	44
Other	53	13	34

Table 66

I Look Forward to Retirement as
an Enjoyable Period of My Life

	AGREE	NEUTRAL	DISAGREE
ALL FACULTY	**75%**	**11%**	**14%**
TYPE OF INSTITUTION			
Four Year	73	12	15
Two Year	80	9	11
CARNEGIE CLASSIFICATION			
Research	69	13	18
Doctorate	73	11	16
Comprehensive	75	12	13
Liberal Arts	76	11	13
Two Year	80	9	11
AGE			
Under 40	70	15	15
40 to 49	74	11	15
50 to 59	79	10	11
60 to 64	78	12	10
65 and over	74	7	19
GENDER			
Male	75	11	14
Female	76	11	13
DEPARTMENT			
Biological Sciences	73	13	14
Business/Communications	71	14	14
Education	75	8	17
Engineering	72	11	17
Humanities	75	13	13
Mathematics	71	11	18
Physical Sciences	72	11	17
Social Sciences	74	10	17
Other	84	7	9

Chart 20.   **This Is a Poor Time for Any Young Person to Begin an Academic Career**

(percent agreeing)

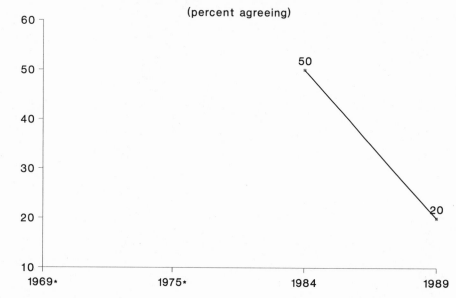

*Data not available

Chart 21.

If Deciding Again, I Would Not
Become a College Teacher
(percent agreeing)

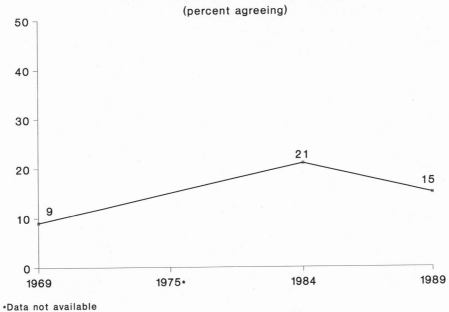

*Data not available

Chart 22.

I Tend to Subordinate All
Aspects of Life to My Work
(percent agreeing)

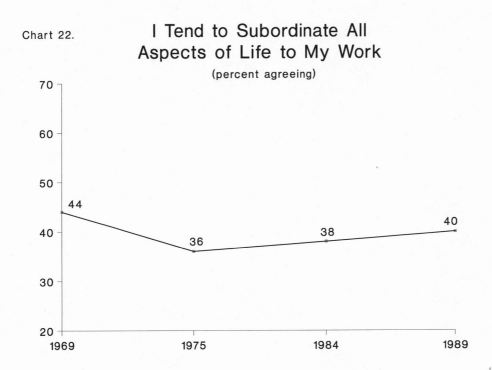

Chart 23. I Hardly Ever Get Time to Give a Piece of Work the Attention It Deserves

(percent agreeing)

70
60
50
40
30
20
50
41
45
43
1969
1975
1984
1989

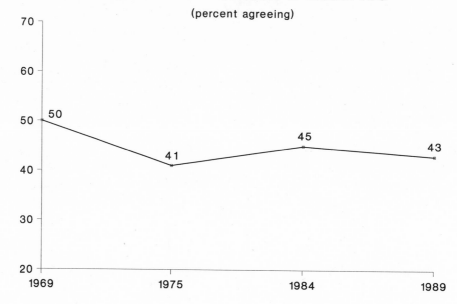

Chart 24. My Job Is the Source of Considerable Personal Strain

(percent agreeing)

70
60
50
40
30
20
43
36
40
44
1969
1975
1984
1989

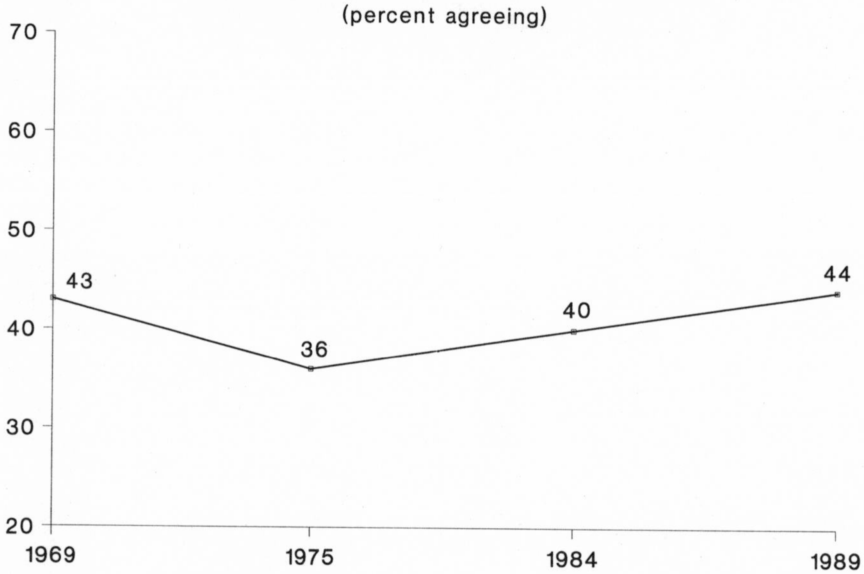

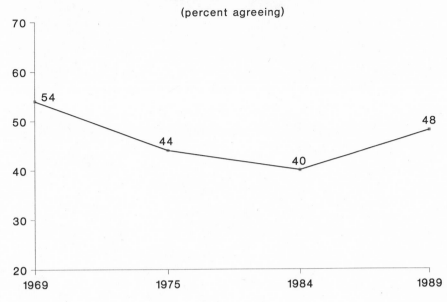

Chart 25.

Would You Rate Your Own Salary as Excellent or Good?

(percent agreeing)

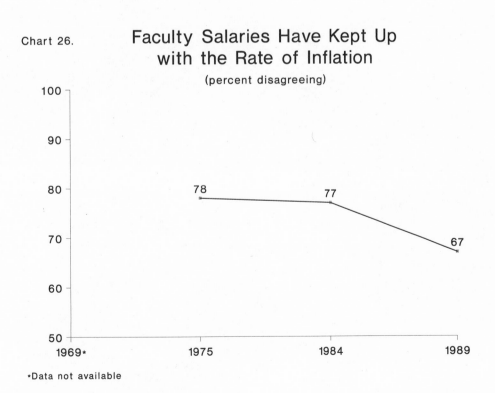

Chart 26.

Faculty Salaries Have Kept Up with the Rate of Inflation

(percent disagreeing)

*Data not available

91

6

Views of the Institution

Faculty satisfaction with their particular institution is closely related to their feelings about a range of key issues:

- administration, including commitment to academic freedom, support of faculty, and management effectiveness;

- the quality of the undergraduate education offered;

- professional issues, such as tenure, job security, and retirement prospects;

- quality of life, including the quality of the intellectual environment, the sense of community, and the degree of identification faculty feel with their discipline, department, and institution;

- financial stability of the institution;

- and the issue of affirmative action.

Faculty have, we suspect, always had mixed feelings about their administrations, and surely there is ambivalence today. Only half the faculty we surveyed believe that their institutions are managed effectively, and two-thirds say administrations are autocratic. They agree that the administrators support academic freedom, yet they rate overall administrative performance only "fair" or "poor."

American professors give relatively good grades to the undergraduate education programs offered at their institution. They believe their college or university is doing a good job in providing undergraduates with an "excellent" or a "better than adequate" general education, and are also doing well in preparing them for a vocation or career. They believe, too, that the places where they work are providing undergraduates with the opportunity to explore a subject in depth. Two-thirds feel that their college or university performs adequately or better in strengthening the students' values.

Although faculty are not worried about a loss of jobs due to lack of funds in the near future, they suggest that administrations may be resorting to other measures to save money on faculty salaries. For example, 58 percent of responding faculty members report that the number of part-time and adjunct faculty has increased over the past five years. Based on other comments received, we believe this hiring practice may contribute at least in part to negative views by faculty of their administration.

According to our most recent survey, about half the faculty feel tenure is harder to get than it was five years ago; this is a decline from 68 percent in 1984.

We also found that in spite of the use of part-time and adjunct instructors, and even though tenure is still difficult to achieve, only 20 percent of respondents believe that many young professors will leave because of a shortage of tenure positions.

On the more personal matter of retirement, 56 percent agree that their institution provides the conditions and support for them to retire with dignity.

Faculty are evenly split between those who rate the quality of life on their campus "good" or "excellent" and those who rate it only "fair" or "poor." Liberal Arts and two-year faculty are happier on this general issue, and positive ratings also rise with age. Men give higher positive ratings than do women. A majority of today's faculty consider the intellectual environment on campus to be "fair" or "poor." But the ratings are best at Research and Liberal Arts institutions.

The absence of community is disturbing. Sixty-three percent of the faculty say the sense of community at their institution is only "fair" or "poor." As might be expected, faculty at Liberal Arts and two-year colleges give the highest ratings to the sense of community, and those at Research and Doctorate-granting institutions give the lowest.

We found that, once again, faculty identify strongly with their academic discipline, less so with their department, and still less with their institution. We believe it is significant, however, that the number of faculty who say their college or university is "very important" to them has increased dramatically since 1984, rising from 29 to 40 percent.

Overall, opinions among faculty about college finances are evenly split. Faculty at two-year colleges, however, perceive less serious financial problems at their institutions than do faculty at four-year institutions.

The results of affirmative action efforts on campus are felt to be satisfactory by half the faculty, with 21 percent reporting neutral responses, and 30 percent reporting dissatisfaction with the results. Older faculty and faculty at two-year institutions appear to be the most satisfied on this issue.

Table 67

In General, How Do You Feel About Your Institution?

	VERY GOOD PLACE	FAIRLY GOOD PLACE	NOT THE PLACE FOR ME
ALL FACULTY	**49%**	**43%**	**7%**
TYPE OF INSTITUTION			
Four Year	41	49	10
Two Year	65	32	3
CARNEGIE CLASSIFICATION			
Research	42	48	9
Doctorate	37	52	11
Comprehensive	39	51	10
Liberal Arts	50	42	8
Two Year	65	32	3
AGE			
Under 40	37	52	11
40 to 49	47	45	8
50 to 59	53	42	5
60 to 64	59	36	5
65 and over	63	28	9
GENDER			
Male	49	44	7
Female	50	42	8
DEPARTMENT			
Biological Sciences	50	41	9
Business/Communications	51	42	7
Education	47	46	7
Engineering	43	49	8
Humanities	46	44	10
Mathematics	57	38	5
Physical Sciences	45	51	4
Social Sciences	47	44	9
Other	55	41	5

Table 68

The Administration Here Supports Academic Freedom

	AGREE	NEUTRAL	DISAGREE
ALL FACULTY	**67%**	**16%**	**17%**
TYPE OF INSTITUTION			
Four Year	64	17	19
Two Year	74	12	14
CARNEGIE CLASSIFICATION			
Research	63	20	17
Doctorate	61	19	20
Comprehensive	62	16	21
Liberal Arts	75	11	14
Two Year	74	12	14
AGE			
Under 40	60	22	19
40 to 49	64	16	20
50 to 59	70	14	16
60 to 64	76	12	12
65 and over	75	15	11
GENDER			
Male	68	15	16
Female	65	16	18
DEPARTMENT			
Biological Sciences	67	15	17
Business/Communications	64	19	17
Education	69	14	17
Engineering	57	30	14
Humanities	67	14	19
Mathematics	73	15	12
Physical Sciences	63	15	22
Social Sciences	67	13	20
Other	73	15	12

Table 69

Undergraduates at <u>My Institution</u> Are Not Getting as Good an Education as They Did Five Years Ago

	AGREE	NEUTRAL	DISAGREE
ALL FACULTY	**18%**	**24%**	**58%**
TYPE OF INSTITUTION			
Four Year	17	27	56
Two Year	20	17	62
CARNEGIE CLASSIFICATION			
Research	17	32	51
Doctorate	18	27	55
Comprehensive	19	23	58
Liberal Arts	14	21	65
Two Year	20	17	62
AGE			
Under 40	14	36	50
40 to 49	17	23	60
50 to 59	21	19	60
60 to 64	20	18	62
65 and over	22	22	56
GENDER			
Male	18	24	58
Female	19	23	58
DEPARTMENT			
Biological Sciences	17	21	62
Business/Communications	19	21	60
Education	11	32	57
Engineering	21	29	50
Humanities	22	21	57
Mathematics	11	22	67
Physical Sciences	20	27	53
Social Sciences	17	26	57
Other	18	22	60

Table 70

Rate the Performance of Your Institution
in Providing Undergraduates with a General Education

	EXCELLENT	BETTER THAN ADEQUATE	ADEQUATE	LESS THAN ADEQUATE	POOR
ALL FACULTY	**37%**	**38%**	**19%**	**5%**	**1%**
TYPE OF INSTITUTION					
Four Year	29	40	22	6	2
Two Year	53	32	12	3	0
CARNEGIE CLASSIFICATION					
Research	24	38	27	7	4
Doctorate	28	41	24	6	2
Comprehensive	29	44	20	6	2
Liberal Arts	51	33	12	3	1
Two Year	53	32	12	3	0
AGE					
Under 40	32	39	22	6	2
40 to 49	34	39	19	6	2
50 to 59	40	38	16	4	1
60 to 64	44	30	20	5	2
65 and over	49	28	16	5	2
GENDER					
Male	36	38	19	6	2
Female	40	37	18	4	1
DEPARTMENT					
Biological Sciences	39	33	21	5	2
Business/Communications	37	38	19	5	1
Education	32	39	23	3	3
Engineering	30	37	27	4	3
Humanities	34	39	19	6	2
Mathematics	40	38	15	6	1
Physical Sciences	32	44	19	5	0
Social Sciences	36	37	18	6	2
Other	46	35	14	4	1

Table 71

Rate the Performance of Your Institution
in Preparing Undergraduates for a Career

	EXCELLENT	BETTER THAN ADEQUATE	ADEQUATE	LESS THAN ADEQUATE	POOR
ALL FACULTY	**35%**	**40%**	**20%**	**4%**	**1%**
TYPE OF INSTITUTION					
Four Year	22	46	25	6	2
Two Year	59	30	10	2	0
CARNEGIE CLASSIFICATION					
Research	19	43	28	7	3
Doctorate	23	46	25	4	1
Comprehensive	23	48	22	5	1
Liberal Arts	27	44	23	4	2
Two Year	59	30	10	2	0
AGE					
Under 40	30	37	26	6	2
40 to 49	33	40	21	4	1
50 to 59	36	43	16	3	1
60 to 64	40	41	15	3	1
65 and over	47	29	16	5	2
GENDER					
Male	32	41	21	5	2
Female	42	37	17	3	0
DEPARTMENT					
Biological Sciences	34	37	23	4	2
Business/Communications	39	41	15	4	2
Education	29	44	21	5	1
Engineering	31	45	16	6	3
Humanities	28	45	23	3	0
Mathematics	32	41	20	6	1
Physical Sciences	24	49	23	2	1
Social Sciences	29	39	23	7	2
Other	52	30	15	3	1

Table 72

Rate the Performance of Your Institution in Providing Undergraduates with the Opportunity to Explore a Subject in Depth

	EXCELLENT	BETTER THAN ADEQUATE	ADEQUATE	LESS THAN ADEQUATE	POOR
ALL FACULTY	**29%**	**36%**	**23%**	**9%**	**3%**
TYPE OF INSTITUTION					
Four Year	32	39	20	7	2
Two Year	24	31	29	13	4
CARNEGIE CLASSIFICATION					
Research	34	35	20	9	2
Doctorate	32	38	22	7	1
Comprehensive	27	44	21	7	2
Liberal Arts	41	36	16	6	1
Two Year	24	31	29	13	4
AGE					
Under 40	22	38	26	12	2
40 to 49	29	35	24	9	3
50 to 59	30	36	22	8	2
60 to 64	33	38	21	5	2
65 and over	33	30	21	12	4
GENDER					
Male	29	36	22	10	2
Female	29	35	26	8	3
DEPARTMENT					
Biological Sciences	27	36	25	8	4
Business/Communications	26	36	28	7	2
Education	32	39	24	4	1
Engineering	25	39	23	9	5
Humanities	30	34	22	11	3
Mathematics	24	39	21	13	4
Physical Sciences	35	34	14	12	4
Social Sciences	26	35	25	11	2
Other	32	38	23	6	2

Table 73

Rate the Performance of Your Institution
in Strengthening the Values of Undergraduates

	EXCELLENT	BETTER THAN ADEQUATE	ADEQUATE	LESS THAN ADEQUATE	POOR
ALL FACULTY	13%	24%	36%	21%	6%
TYPE OF INSTITUTION					
Four Year	12	22	35	23	8
Two Year	16	27	36	16	4
CARNEGIE CLASSIFICATION					
Research	7	17	39	27	10
Doctorate	12	20	37	24	7
Comprehensive	10	24	35	24	7
Liberal Arts	34	36	20	8	2
Two Year	16	27	36	16	4
AGE					
Under 40	11	19	39	23	8
40 to 49	13	24	34	22	7
50 to 59	13	26	37	19	5
60 to 64	15	27	34	19	5
65 and over	21	23	31	21	3
GENDER					
Male	13	23	37	21	7
Female	15	26	33	22	5
DEPARTMENT					
Biological Sciences	15	23	37	18	7
Business/Communications	15	24	33	22	7
Education	14	20	40	21	6
Engineering	6	22	41	20	10
Humanities	14	23	33	22	8
Mathematics	8	33	32	18	9
Physical Sciences	11	24	39	20	7
Social Sciences	11	20	38	24	7
Other	16	27	36	18	2

101

Table 74

Rate the Performance of Your Institution in Creating
Opportunities for Undergraduates to Engage in Public Service

	EXCELLENT	BETTER THAN ADEQUATE	ADEQUATE	LESS THAN ADEQUATE	POOR
ALL FACULTY	10%	20%	36%	25%	9%
TYPE OF INSTITUTION					
Four Year	9	20	36	26	9
Two Year	12	19	36	24	9
CARNEGIE CLASSIFICATION					
Research	6	17	38	27	12
Doctorate	8	20	36	27	10
Comprehensive	9	20	37	27	7
Liberal Arts	21	32	27	16	4
Two Year	12	19	36	24	9
AGE					
Under 40	9	18	39	26	9
40 to 49	11	18	35	26	10
50 to 59	8	19	38	27	8
60 to 64	13	26	32	21	8
65 and over	15	24	33	21	7
GENDER					
Male	9	20	38	25	9
Female	12	19	32	27	9
DEPARTMENT					
Biological Sciences	14	14	35	29	8
Business/Communications	9	17	34	30	9
Education	12	16	37	23	11
Engineering	4	19	37	25	15
Humanities	10	20	35	24	10
Mathematics	3	22	45	23	7
Physical Sciences	7	18	39	26	10
Social Sciences	11	24	34	24	8
Other	12	21	37	23	6

Table 75

In the Next Five Years, I Expect
That Some of the Tenured Faculty Here
Will Lose Their Jobs Due to Lack of Funds

	AGREE	NEUTRAL	DISAGREE
ALL FACULTY	**11%**	**16%**	**73%**
TYPE OF INSTITUTION			
Four Year	11	14	74
Two Year	11	18	71
CARNEGIE CLASSIFICATION			
Research	12	14	74
Doctorate	10	13	77
Comprehensive	12	15	74
Liberal Arts	12	15	73
Two Year	11	18	71
AGE			
Under 40	11	16	72
40 to 49	11	15	75
50 to 59	12	15	73
60 to 64	9	15	75
65 and over	15	24	62
GENDER			
Male	11	15	74
Female	11	16	72
DEPARTMENT			
Biological Sciences	14	15	71
Business/Communications	8	15	77
Education	15	11	74
Engineering	10	22	68
Humanities	11	16	73
Mathematics	10	14	76
Physical Sciences	9	13	78
Social Sciences	7	13	80
Other	18	19	63

Table 76

Many Young Faculty Members at This
Institution Will Leave Because It Is Tenured In

	AGREE	NEUTRAL	DISAGREE
ALL FACULTY	**20%**	**22%**	**59%**
TYPE OF INSTITUTION			
Four Year	22	18	60
Two Year	14	29	57
CARNEGIE CLASSIFICATION			
Research	21	16	63
Doctorate	22	18	60
Comprehensive	23	19	58
Liberal Arts	26	21	53
Two Year	14	29	57
AGE			
Under 40	23	29	48
40 to 49	17	19	64
50 to 59	21	19	60
60 to 64	15	24	61
65 and over	21	28	51
GENDER			
Male	19	22	59
Female	21	21	58
DEPARTMENT			
Biological Sciences	17	14	69
Business/Communications	19	20	60
Education	22	17	61
Engineering	13	31	56
Humanities	23	21	56
Mathematics	12	25	63
Physical Sciences	13	18	68
Social Sciences	19	17	64
Other	22	28	50

Table 77

I Am Satisfied with the Results
of Affirmative Action at This Institution

	AGREE	NEUTRAL	DISAGREE
ALL FACULTY	**49%**	**21%**	**30%**
TYPE OF INSTITUTION			
Four Year	46	22	32
Two Year	55	20	25
CARNEGIE CLASSIFICATION			
Research	44	20	36
Doctorate	47	22	31
Comprehensive	48	22	29
Liberal Arts	46	22	31
Two Year	55	20	25
AGE			
Under 40	41	27	32
40 to 49	47	19	34
50 to 59	53	21	26
60 to 64	56	19	25
65 and over	55	26	19
GENDER			
Male	50	23	27
Female	48	17	35
DEPARTMENT			
Biological Sciences	52	22	27
Business/Communications	50	20	30
Education	52	14	34
Engineering	50	31	18
Humanities	45	22	33
Mathematics	43	26	31
Physical Sciences	50	26	23
Social Sciences	47	18	35
Other	56	20	24

Table 78

My Institution Provides the Conditions
and Support for Faculty to Retire with Dignity

	AGREE	NEUTRAL	DISAGREE
ALL FACULTY	**56%**	**26%**	**18%**
TYPE OF INSTITUTION			
Four Year	52	28	20
Two Year	65	20	15
CARNEGIE CLASSIFICATION			
Research	52	30	18
Doctorate	52	28	20
Comprehensive	51	28	21
Liberal Arts	56	23	20
Two Year	65	20	15
AGE			
Under 40	46	36	18
40 to 49	54	28	18
50 to 59	61	21	18
60 to 64	62	17	21
65 and over	64	18	17
GENDER			
Male	56	27	17
Female	58	23	19
DEPARTMENT			
Biological Sciences	59	21	20
Business/Communications	56	26	17
Education	54	26	20
Engineering	47	40	14
Humanities	56	24	20
Mathematics	60	31	10
Physical Sciences	53	32	15
Social Sciences	52	26	21
Other	63	21	16

106

Table 79

How Would You Rate the Administration at Your Institution?

	EXCELLENT	GOOD	FAIR	POOR
ALL FACULTY	**6%**	**30%**	**35%**	**29%**
TYPE OF INSTITUTION				
Four Year	4	27	36	32
Two Year	9	36	34	21
CARNEGIE CLASSIFICATION				
Research	4	24	39	34
Doctorate	4	26	36	34
Comprehensive	4	28	34	33
Liberal Arts	9	38	33	20
Two Year	9	36	34	21
AGE				
Under 40	4	27	40	29
40 to 49	5	30	34	31
50 to 59	7	30	36	27
60 to 64	9	34	30	26
65 and over	5	34	32	29
GENDER				
Male	6	30	34	30
Female	7	31	38	24
DEPARTMENT				
Biological Sciences	4	20	42	33
Business/Communications	7	30	35	28
Education	4	33	33	30
Engineering	3	26	36	35
Humanities	4	29	36	31
Mathematics	11	33	35	22
Physical Sciences	3	27	37	32
Social Sciences	5	28	33	35
Other	9	38	34	18

Table 80

Do You Feel That the Administration
of Your Institution Is Autocratic or Democratic?

	VERY AUTOCRATIC	SOMEWHAT AUTOCRATIC	SOMEWHAT DEMOCRATIC	VERY DEMOCRATIC
ALL FACULTY	**30%**	**39%**	**25%**	**6%**
TYPE OF INSTITUTION				
Four Year	32	40	24	5
Two Year	28	39	28	6
CARNEGIE CLASSIFICATION				
Research	31	41	23	5
Doctorate	33	42	22	4
Comprehensive	34	39	22	4
Liberal Arts	22	31	34	13
Two Year	28	39	28	6
AGE				
Under 40	36	40	22	2
40 to 49	31	38	24	6
50 to 59	28	40	25	6
60 to 64	27	36	32	5
65 and over	27	42	23	8
GENDER				
Male	30	40	25	6
Female	31	38	25	6
DEPARTMENT				
Biological Sciences	38	40	18	4
Business/Communications	33	40	19	7
Education	31	36	24	8
Engineering	26	48	20	7
Humanities	29	39	27	4
Mathematics	21	38	35	6
Physical Sciences	30	39	28	3
Social Sciences	32	38	25	5
Other	28	39	26	6

Table 81

There Are More Part-time and Adjunct Faculty Members at This Institution Today Than There Were Five Years Ago

	AGREE	NEUTRAL	DISAGREE
ALL FACULTY	**58%**	**20%**	**23%**
TYPE OF INSTITUTION			
Four Year	49	24	27
Two Year	75	11	15
CARNEGIE CLASSIFICATION			
Research	38	30	32
Doctorate	50	26	24
Comprehensive	57	19	24
Liberal Arts	55	21	24
Two Year	75	11	15
AGE			
Under 40	52	29	19
40 to 49	58	18	24
50 to 59	61	18	21
60 to 64	61	15	24
65 and over	54	19	28
GENDER			
Male	56	20	24
Female	63	18	20
DEPARTMENT			
Biological Sciences	55	23	22
Business/Communications	54	19	27
Education	58	18	23
Engineering	30	39	31
Humanities	65	15	20
Mathematics	57	21	23
Physical Sciences	46	27	27
Social Sciences	56	21	23
Other	64	16	20

Table 82

In My Department Tenure Is Now More
Difficult to Achieve Than It Was Five Years Ago

	AGREE	NEUTRAL	DISAGREE
ALL FACULTY	**54%**	**18%**	**28%**
TYPE OF INSTITUTION			
Four Year	63	16	21
Two Year	37	22	41
CARNEGIE CLASSIFICATION			
Research	61	17	23
Doctorate	70	14	16
Comprehensive	65	14	21
Liberal Arts	51	24	25
Two Year	37	22	41
AGE			
Under 40	56	25	19
40 to 49	55	18	27
50 to 59	54	16	30
60 to 64	55	13	31
65 and over	39	20	42
GENDER			
Male	54	19	27
Female	54	16	30
DEPARTMENT			
Biological Sciences	51	19	30
Business/Communications	56	17	27
Education	70	15	15
Engineering	55	27	18
Humanities	54	18	28
Mathematics	45	20	36
Physical Sciences	51	23	26
Social Sciences	56	13	31
Other	53	17	29

Table 83

My Institution Is Managed Effectively

	AGREE	NEUTRAL	DISAGREE
ALL FACULTY	**50%**	**11%**	**39%**
TYPE OF INSTITUTION			
Four Year	44	13	43
Two Year	61	7	31
CARNEGIE CLASSIFICATION			
Research	37	13	49
Doctorate	44	13	43
Comprehensive	46	13	41
Liberal Arts	61	9	30
Two Year	61	7	31
AGE			
Under 40	44	12	44
40 to 49	49	10	41
50 to 59	52	11	37
60 to 64	55	9	36
65 and over	52	15	33
GENDER			
Male	49	11	40
Female	53	10	37
DEPARTMENT			
Biological Sciences	44	9	47
Business/Communications	50	9	41
Education	54	9	37
Engineering	35	18	46
Humanities	49	10	41
Mathematics	57	12	31
Physical Sciences	43	20	36
Social Sciences	44	11	45
Other	60	9	31

Table 84

My Institution Has Serious Financial Problems

	AGREE	NEUTRAL	DISAGREE
ALL FACULTY	**41%**	**19%**	**40%**
TYPE OF INSTITUTION			
Four Year	48	18	34
Two Year	28	21	51
CARNEGIE CLASSIFICATION			
Research	51	20	29
Doctorate	47	18	35
Comprehensive	48	18	34
Liberal Arts	38	12	50
Two Year	28	21	51
AGE			
Under 40	39	23	38
40 to 49	39	19	42
50 to 59	45	15	39
60 to 64	39	20	41
65 and over	42	23	35
GENDER			
Male	42	19	39
Female	39	18	43
DEPARTMENT			
Biological Sciences	46	15	38
Business/Communications	40	22	38
Education	50	10	41
Engineering	42	29	28
Humanities	43	16	41
Mathematics	28	26	46
Physical Sciences	43	25	32
Social Sciences	43	17	40
Other	37	20	43

Table 85

How Would You Rate the Quality
of Life at Your Institution?

	EXCELLENT	GOOD	FAIR	POOR
ALL FACULTY	**11%**	**40%**	**35%**	**15%**
TYPE OF INSTITUTION				
Four Year	9	38	37	17
Two Year	13	44	31	11
CARNEGIE CLASSIFICATION				
Research	10	38	36	16
Doctorate	9	36	37	18
Comprehensive	7	36	39	18
Liberal Arts	13	43	31	13
Two Year	13	44	31	11
AGE				
Under 40	7	37	41	15
40 to 49	10	41	34	16
50 to 59	12	40	34	13
60 to 64	13	40	32	16
65 and over	15	39	34	12
GENDER				
Male	11	42	34	14
Female	10	36	38	16
DEPARTMENT				
Biological Sciences	12	39	35	13
Business/Communications	12	42	32	13
Education	7	35	35	23
Engineering	12	40	29	19
Humanities	7	39	37	17
Mathematics	16	40	33	11
Physical Sciences	6	43	37	15
Social Sciences	11	38	35	16
Other	13	41	36	9

Table 86

How Would You Rate the Intellectual
Environment at Your Institution?

	EXCELLENT	GOOD	FAIR	POOR
ALL FACULTY	**9%**	**36%**	**39%**	**17%**
TYPE OF INSTITUTION				
Four Year	8	34	40	18
Two Year	10	39	37	15
CARNEGIE CLASSIFICATION				
Research	13	39	33	14
Doctorate	5	34	43	18
Comprehensive	3	28	46	22
Liberal Arts	13	39	36	12
Two Year	10	39	37	15
AGE				
Under 40	9	34	38	19
40 to 49	7	33	42	18
50 to 59	9	37	39	16
60 to 64	13	39	35	14
65 and over	10	47	34	9
GENDER				
Male	8	37	38	17
Female	9	34	41	16
DEPARTMENT				
Biological Sciences	7	38	41	14
Business/Communications	9	37	39	16
Education	6	37	37	20
Engineering	9	35	33	24
Humanities	7	32	42	19
Mathematics	14	37	32	18
Physical Sciences	5	33	42	20
Social Sciences	8	32	42	17
Other	12	43	35	10

114

Table 87

How Would You Rate the Sense
of Community at Your Institution?

	EXCELLENT	GOOD	FAIR	POOR
ALL FACULTY	**9%**	**28%**	**33%**	**30%**
TYPE OF INSTITUTION				
Four Year	8	24	35	33
Two Year	10	35	31	24
CARNEGIE CLASSIFICATION				
Research	5	20	36	39
Doctorate	6	24	35	35
Comprehensive	8	24	36	32
Liberal Arts	20	36	27	17
Two Year	10	35	31	24
AGE				
Under 40	8	27	33	32
40 to 49	10	25	34	31
50 to 59	9	29	34	28
60 to 64	9	28	31	32
65 and over	6	33	30	32
GENDER				
Male	8	27	33	31
Female	10	28	33	29
DEPARTMENT				
Biological Sciences	8	27	34	32
Business/Communications	9	36	27	28
Education	8	16	35	41
Engineering	9	26	32	32
Humanities	8	23	35	34
Mathematics	14	38	28	19
Physical Sciences	5	29	40	26
Social Sciences	6	25	35	34
Other	14	30	33	24

Table 88

How Important to You Is Your College or University?

	VERY IMPORTANT	FAIRLY IMPORTANT	FAIRLY UNIMPORTANT	NOT AT ALL IMPORTANT
ALL FACULTY	**40%**	**45%**	**12%**	**2%**
TYPE OF INSTITUTION				
Four Year	35	48	14	3
Two Year	50	41	8	1
CARNEGIE CLASSIFICATION				
Research	30	50	16	4
Doctorate	34	47	16	3
Comprehensive	36	48	13	3
Liberal Arts	52	38	8	1
Two Year	50	41	8	1
AGE				
Under 40	28	53	16	3
40 to 49	37	49	12	2
50 to 59	44	44	9	2
60 to 64	52	34	12	2
65 and over	61	25	10	5
GENDER				
Male	39	45	13	2
Female	43	45	10	2
DEPARTMENT				
Biological Sciences	43	40	13	4
Business/Communications	40	46	13	1
Education	41	46	10	3
Engineering	41	42	16	1
Humanities	38	46	12	3
Mathematics	43	41	15	1
Physical Sciences	32	56	11	1
Social Sciences	36	45	16	3
Other	48	44	7	1

Table 89

How Important to You Is Your Academic Discipline?

	VERY IMPORTANT	FAIRLY IMPORTANT	FAIRLY UNIMPORTANT	NOT AT ALL IMPORTANT
ALL FACULTY	**77%**	**20%**	**2%**	**0%**
TYPE OF INSTITUTION				
Four Year	76	22	2	0
Two Year	81	17	2	0
CARNEGIE CLASSIFICATION				
Research	77	20	2	1
Doctorate	75	23	2	0
Comprehensive	75	23	2	0
Liberal Arts	76	21	2	0
Two Year	81	17	2	0
AGE				
Under 40	77	20	3	1
40 to 49	75	23	2	0
50 to 59	77	20	2	0
60 to 64	84	16	0	0
65 and over	85	13	2	0
GENDER				
Male	75	22	2	0
Female	82	16	1	0
DEPARTMENT				
Biological Sciences	82	17	0	0
Business/Communications	71	24	4	1
Education	81	18	1	0
Engineering	75	23	2	0
Humanities	81	17	1	0
Mathematics	71	27	1	0
Physical Sciences	78	21	1	0
Social Sciences	70	24	5	1
Other	82	18	1	0

Table 90

How Important to You Is Your Department?

	VERY IMPORTANT	FAIRLY IMPORTANT	FAIRLY UNIMPORTANT	NOT AT ALL IMPORTANT
ALL FACULTY	**53%**	**37%**	**8%**	**1%**
TYPE OF INSTITUTION				
Four Year	50	38	10	2
Two Year	58	35	6	1
CARNEGIE CLASSIFICATION				
Research	47	39	11	2
Doctorate	48	41	9	2
Comprehensive	52	37	9	1
Liberal Arts	58	35	5	1
Two Year	58	35	6	1
AGE				
Under 40	45	44	10	1
40 to 49	52	38	8	2
50 to 59	55	35	8	1
60 to 64	59	33	7	1
65 and over	63	26	9	2
GENDER				
Male	52	38	9	1
Female	57	35	7	1
DEPARTMENT				
Biological Sciences	55	34	8	3
Business/Communications	52	41	6	0
Education	49	38	12	1
Engineering	50	43	7	0
Humanities	52	37	10	2
Mathematics	53	37	10	1
Physical Sciences	51	39	8	2
Social Sciences	47	38	12	3
Other	62	32	5	0

Table 91

How Important to You Are National or
International Societies in Your Discipline?

	VERY IMPORTANT	FAIRLY IMPORTANT	FAIRLY UNIMPORTANT	NOT AT ALL IMPORTANT
ALL FACULTY	**18%**	**39%**	**32%**	**11%**
TYPE OF INSTITUTION				
Four Year	21	42	28	9
Two Year	13	32	40	15
CARNEGIE CLASSIFICATION				
Research	26	43	24	8
Doctorate	21	42	29	7
Comprehensive	19	41	30	10
Liberal Arts	13	43	33	11
Two Year	13	32	40	15
AGE				
Under 40	19	44	30	7
40 to 49	16	39	33	12
50 to 59	19	36	33	11
60 to 64	22	36	31	12
65 and over	26	35	28	11
GENDER				
Male	17	37	33	13
Female	22	41	31	6
DEPARTMENT				
Biological Sciences	23	37	28	12
Business/Communications	14	36	39	12
Education	26	53	18	3
Engineering	20	46	28	6
Humanities	16	35	35	14
Mathematics	15	34	44	8
Physical Sciences	12	49	30	9
Social Sciences	18	38	33	11
Other	24	38	28	10

Table 92

How Has Departmental Morale Changed over the Past Five Years?

	WAS NOT TEACHING	BETTER	ABOUT THE SAME	WORSE
ALL FACULTY	**10%**	**31%**	**28%**	**32%**
TYPE OF INSTITUTION				
Four Year	12	33	25	31
Two Year	6	28	33	33
CARNEGIE CLASSIFICATION				
Research	11	30	26	33
Doctorate	12	34	19	34
Comprehensive	11	34	25	30
Liberal Arts	16	35	28	21
Two Year	6	28	33	33
AGE				
Under 40	33	26	17	24
40 to 49	9	34	25	32
50 to 59	2	30	34	34
60 to 64	3	29	33	36
65 and over	0	39	33	28
GENDER				
Male	9	32	29	30
Female	13	30	23	35
DEPARTMENT				
Biological Sciences	8	29	31	31
Business/Communications	13	28	30	29
Education	16	28	21	35
Engineering	13	32	24	30
Humanities	7	34	27	32
Mathematics	10	29	34	27
Physical Sciences	10	29	32	29
Social Sciences	9	32	30	28
Other	9	30	23	38

Chart 27.

In General, My Institution
Is a Very Good Place
(percent agreeing)

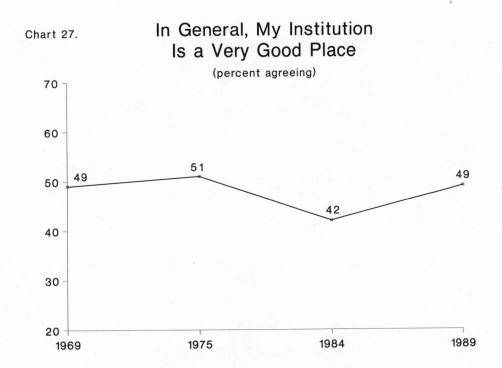

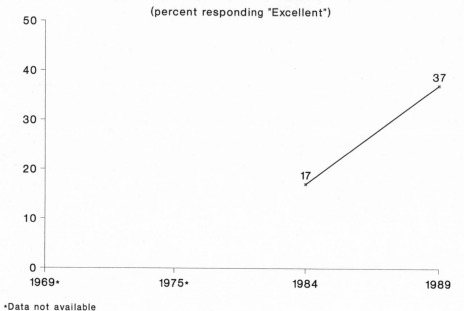

Chart 28.   Performance of Institution in Providing
Undergraduates with General Education

(percent responding "Excellent")

*Data not available

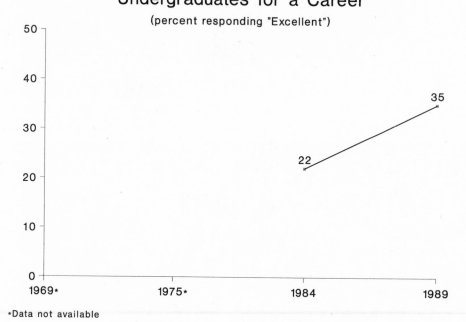

Chart 29.   Performance of Institution in Preparing
Undergraduates for a Career

(percent responding "Excellent")

*Data not available

122

Chart 30.
Some Faculty Will Lose Jobs Due
to Lack of Funds
(percent agreeing)

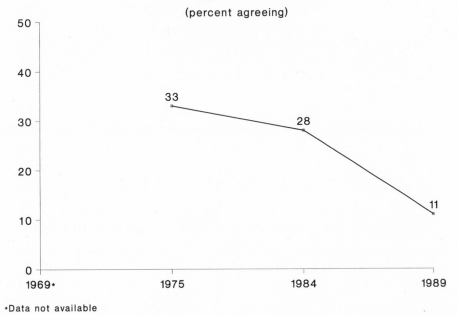

50

40

33

30

28

20

11

10

0

1969*   1975   1984   1989

*Data not available

Chart 31.
Administration at Your Institution
Is Fair or Poor
(percent agreeing)

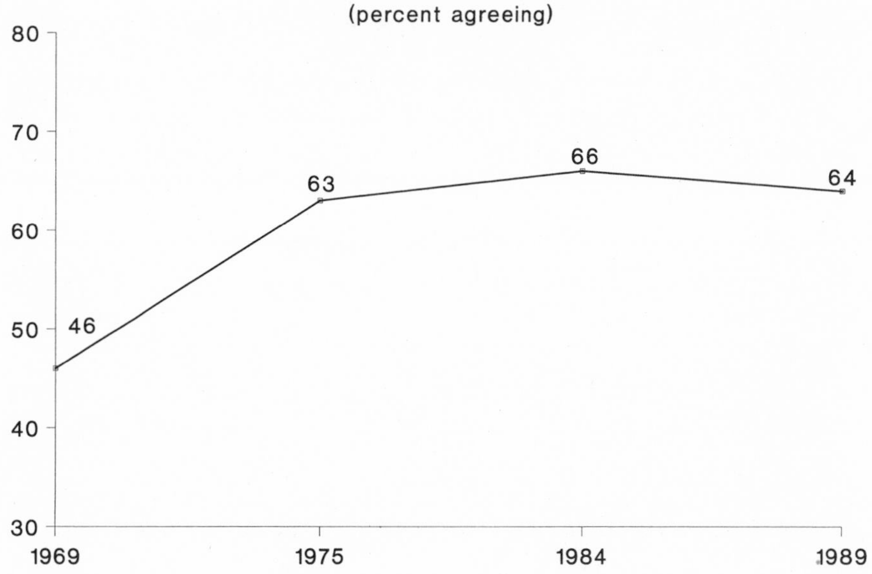

80

70

66

64

63

60

50   46

40

30

1969   1975   1984   1989

Chart 32.

Administration of Institution Is
Somewhat or Very Autocratic
(percent agreeing)

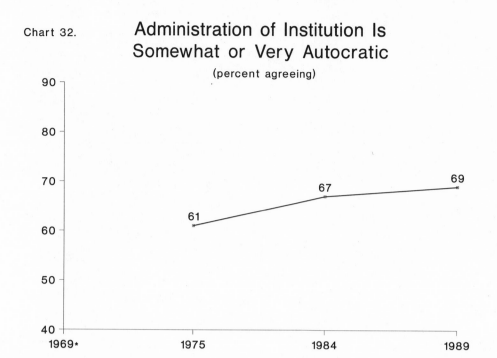

*Data not available

Chart 33.

Tenure Is More Difficult to Achieve
Than Five Years Ago
(percent agreeing)

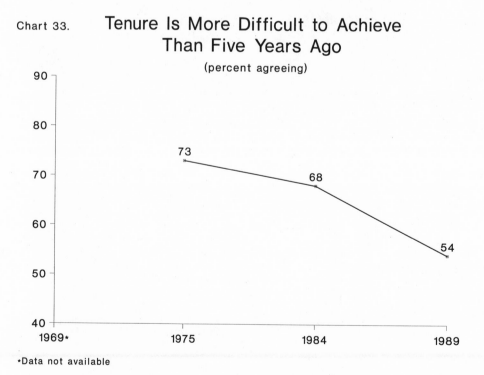

*Data not available

124

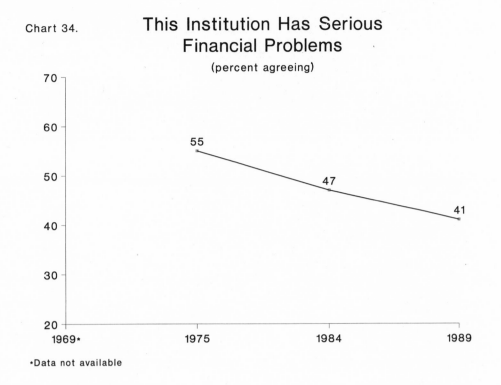

Chart 34.

This Institution Has Serious
Financial Problems
(percent agreeing)

*Data not available

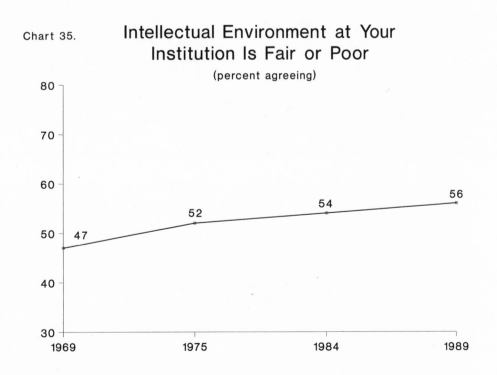

Chart 35.

Intellectual Environment at Your
Institution Is Fair or Poor
(percent agreeing)

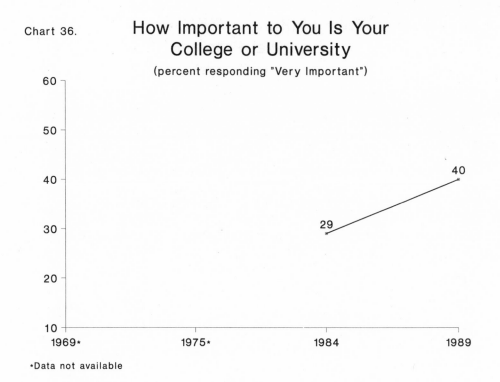

Chart 36.

How Important to You Is Your
College or University
(percent responding "Very Important")

*Data not available

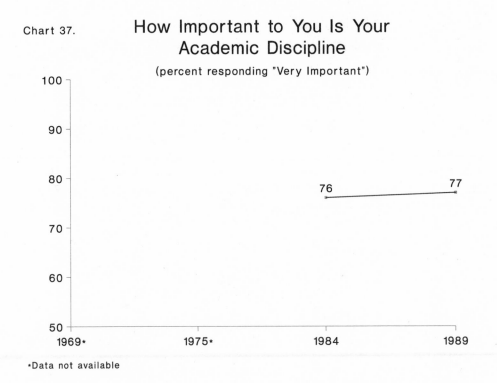

Chart 37.

How Important to You Is Your
Academic Discipline
(percent responding "Very Important")

*Data not available

Chart 38.

How Important to You
Is Your Department

(percent responding "Very Important")

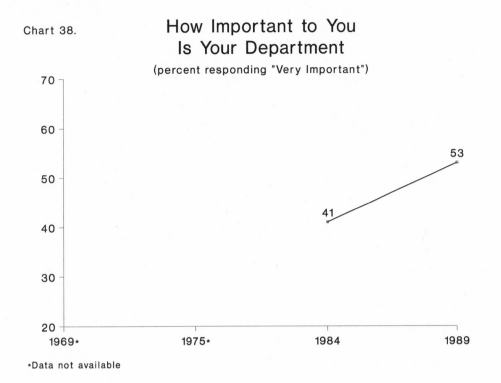

*Data not available

Chart 39.

How Has Departmental Morale
Changed Over the Past Five Years

(percent responding "Better")

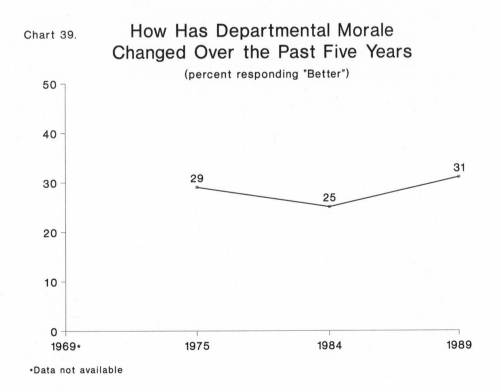

*Data not available

7

Participation in Decision-making

The involvement of faculty in the governance process is essential to the development of an effective learning community. This survey, like others before it, reveals great diversity in the extent of faculty participation in decision-making. The size of the institution largely determines the nature and extent of faculty involvement in policy decisions, with more participation seen by a greater proportion of the faculty at smaller institutions.

As might be expected, faculty participation at the departmental level approaches 90 percent and is relatively uniform across academic rank and gender. Seventy-three percent say they have a lot of opportunity to influence policy at the departmental level.

A third of the faculty report participating as well in campus-wide faculty committee meetings. The degree of actual influence at this level, however, is necessarily more restricted. One is appointed or elected to many of these decision-making bodies, and membership is a small percentage of all eligible faculty.

Faculty, both in the data and in the written comments, expressed ambivalence about their ability to influence decision-making at their institutions. One professor in the fine arts at a Comprehensive university expressed his frustration with the inability to affect policy. "Communication from the upper administration downward is seriously inadequate; similarly, there is no system of assuring faculty input into decisions—and no visible way in the future for the faculty to become meaningfully involved in our own destiny." But an assistant professor in the physical sciences at a Liberal Arts college took her peers to task in her comments to us:

> Faculty members here are not helpless in changing policies and correcting deficiencies. There is much room for improvement here, but too many faculty members are totally passive. Faculty members who "care" can bring about great positive change—energy and enthusiasm are not met with disapproval here.

Table 93

How Much Opportunity Do You Have
to Influence the Policies of Your Institution?

	A LOT	SOME	NONE
ALL FACULTY	**20%**	**49%**	**30%**
TYPE OF INSTITUTION			
Four Year	19	47	34
Two Year	22	54	24
CARNEGIE CLASSIFICATION			
Research	14	47	39
Doctorate	16	46	37
Comprehensive	21	47	32
Liberal Arts	38	49	13
Two Year	22	54	24
AGE			
Under 40	11	45	45
40 to 49	22	49	29
50 to 59	23	52	25
60 to 64	22	49	28
65 and over	18	51	31
GENDER			
Male	21	49	30
Female	20	49	32
DEPARTMENT			
Biological Sciences	19	48	33
Business/Communications	19	50	31
Education	26	44	30
Engineering	10	46	43
Humanities	22	49	28
Mathematics	25	47	28
Physical Sciences	18	56	26
Social Sciences	19	49	33
Other	20	50	29

Table 94

How Much Opportunity Do You Have
to Influence the Policies of Your Department?

	A LOT	SOME	NONE
ALL FACULTY	**73%**	**23%**	**4%**
TYPE OF INSTITUTION			
Four Year	72	24	5
Two Year	76	21	3
CARNEGIE CLASSIFICATION			
Research	67	27	6
Doctorate	66	28	6
Comprehensive	75	21	4
Liberal Arts	87	11	2
Two Year	76	21	3
AGE			
Under 40	63	32	5
40 to 49	77	19	4
50 to 59	74	23	3
60 to 64	80	17	3
65 and over	65	27	8
GENDER			
Male	74	22	3
Female	71	24	5
DEPARTMENT			
Biological Sciences	65	29	6
Business/Communications	77	19	4
Education	74	21	5
Engineering	68	25	7
Humanities	72	24	3
Mathematics	73	26	2
Physical Sciences	78	20	2
Social Sciences	72	24	4
Other	75	21	4

Table 95

Indicate the Extent to Which You Participate
in Departmental Faculty Meetings at Your Institution

	NEVER	RARELY	SOMETIMES	OFTEN
ALL FACULTY	**1%**	**3%**	**8%**	**88%**
TYPE OF INSTITUTION				
Four Year	1	2	8	89
Two Year	1	3	10	85
CARNEGIE CLASSIFICATION				
Research	2	2	8	89
Doctorate	1	3	9	87
Comprehensive	1	2	8	88
Liberal Arts	1	2	4	93
Two Year	1	3	10	85
AGE				
Under 40	1	3	11	84
40 to 49	1	1	7	90
50 to 59	1	3	7	89
60 to 64	1	3	10	85
65 and over	5	5	11	78
GENDER				
Male	1	3	10	86
Female	1	2	6	91
DEPARTMENT				
Biological Sciences	1	3	8	89
Business/Communications	2	2	9	87
Education	1	2	6	90
Engineering	1	2	8	89
Humanities	1	3	8	87
Mathematics	0	1	7	92
Physical Sciences	2	2	6	89
Social Sciences	2	3	10	85
Other	1	2	9	88

Table 96

Indicate the Extent to Which You Participate in
Campus-wide Faculty Committee Meetings at Your Institution

	NEVER	RARELY	SOMETIMES	OFTEN
ALL FACULTY	**17%**	**19%**	**31%**	**33%**
TYPE OF INSTITUTION				
Four Year	19	19	30	33
Two Year	12	21	35	33
CARNEGIE CLASSIFICATION				
Research	27	24	31	19
Doctorate	22	21	31	26
Comprehensive	14	16	30	39
Liberal Arts	6	8	21	66
Two Year	12	21	35	33
AGE				
Under 40	32	17	26	25
40 to 49	14	19	32	35
50 to 59	11	21	33	35
60 to 64	16	16	35	33
65 and over	19	23	34	24
GENDER				
Male	17	21	32	30
Female	16	14	30	40
DEPARTMENT				
Biological Sciences	14	26	29	31
Business/Communications	19	15	32	33
Education	14	17	31	38
Engineering	24	24	30	23
Humanities	15	20	29	36
Mathematics	15	22	30	33
Physical Sciences	17	24	34	25
Social Sciences	16	16	33	35
Other	17	19	34	30

133

Table 97

Indicate the Extent to Which You Participate in Faculty Senate
(or Comparable Campus-wide Faculty Unit) Meetings at Your Institution

	NEVER	RARELY	SOMETIMES	OFTEN
ALL FACULTY	**31%**	**26%**	**21%**	**22%**
TYPE OF INSTITUTION				
Four Year	38	23	17	22
Two Year	19	31	30	20
CARNEGIE CLASSIFICATION				
Research	46	26	15	12
Doctorate	40	25	19	16
Comprehensive	36	22	17	25
Liberal Arts	10	11	21	58
Two Year	19	31	30	20
AGE				
Under 40	47	24	13	16
40 to 49	32	24	21	24
50 to 59	25	29	24	22
60 to 64	28	25	29	18
65 and over	28	25	24	23
GENDER				
Male	33	27	20	20
Female	27	23	24	26
DEPARTMENT				
Biological Sciences	35	25	17	23
Business/Communications	34	24	21	21
Education	28	25	22	25
Engineering	41	28	17	14
Humanities	29	25	21	26
Mathematics	29	25	24	22
Physical Sciences	34	27	24	15
Social Sciences	32	24	21	22
Other	30	28	25	17

Table 98

Indicate the Extent to Which You Participate in
Administrative Advisory Committee Meetings at Your Institution

	NEVER	RARELY	SOMETIMES	OFTEN
ALL FACULTY	**37%**	**20%**	**24%**	**19%**
TYPE OF INSTITUTION				
Four Year	38	19	23	20
Two Year	34	23	25	18
CARNEGIE CLASSIFICATION				
Research	39	18	25	18
Doctorate	39	18	22	20
Comprehensive	40	20	22	17
Liberal Arts	29	19	21	31
Two Year	34	23	25	18
AGE				
Under 40	50	19	18	13
40 to 49	34	20	25	21
50 to 59	34	22	26	19
60 to 64	33	21	25	20
65 and over	41	20	20	19
GENDER				
Male	35	22	25	18
Female	39	18	21	22
DEPARTMENT				
Biological Sciences	35	22	26	18
Business/Communications	34	21	26	19
Education	31	18	25	26
Engineering	43	24	21	11
Humanities	37	19	24	20
Mathematics	41	16	26	17
Physical Sciences	37	25	22	16
Social Sciences	37	24	19	20
Other	37	19	24	20

8

General Observations

Faculty are apprehensive about the future of the nation. The pessimism regarding the nation's future cuts across all institutional, disciplinary, and gender groups.

Over half of our respondents describe themselves as moderately liberal or liberal politically, with a quarter describing themselves as moderately conservative or conservative. A small cluster describe themselves as "middle of the road."

Today's faculty are about equally divided about the capacity of higher education to shape a better society. Faculty expressing the least confidence in higher learning are those over 60, and those in the social sciences.

On a related matter, 60 percent of responding faculty reject the notion that colleges and universities are creating, in society today, an overtrained work force.

Finally, nearly 30 percent of the faculty agreed that "the abolition of faculty tenure would, on the whole, improve the quality of American higher education." Not surprising, this feeling was most prevalent among younger faculty members. Other findings indicate that faculty are more disturbed over the criteria used to judge tenure worthiness than over tenure itself. This is an important issue for the professoriate, since it deals with the balance between teaching and research and, of course, the most important factor of all—the preservation of academic freedom.

Table 99

I Am Apprehensive About the Future of This Country

	AGREE	NEUTRAL	DISAGREE
ALL FACULTY	**63%**	**10%**	**26%**
TYPE OF INSTITUTION			
Four Year	64	10	26
Two Year	63	10	27
CARNEGIE CLASSIFICATION			
Research	63	13	24
Doctorate	63	9	28
Comprehensive	64	8	28
Liberal Arts	66	9	25
Two Year	63	10	27
AGE			
Under 40	67	13	20
40 to 49	64	10	26
50 to 59	61	9	30
60 to 64	62	9	29
65 and over	69	7	24
GENDER			
Male	63	10	27
Female	64	10	26
DEPARTMENT			
Biological Sciences	68	10	22
Business/Communications	57	8	35
Education	53	8	38
Engineering	59	17	25
Humanities	73	10	18
Mathematics	62	15	23
Physical Sciences	64	11	25
Social Sciences	67	9	24
Other	56	11	34

Table 100

I Am Less Confident Today Than I Used to Be About the Capacities of Higher Education to Help Make a Better Society

	AGREE	NEUTRAL	DISAGREE
ALL FACULTY	**42%**	**17%**	**41%**
TYPE OF INSTITUTION			
Four Year	43	18	39
Two Year	42	14	44
CARNEGIE CLASSIFICATION			
Research	41	22	37
Doctorate	40	19	41
Comprehensive	46	15	39
Liberal Arts	39	16	45
Two Year	42	14	44
AGE			
Under 40	39	19	41
40 to 49	41	16	43
50 to 59	42	18	41
60 to 64	51	16	33
65 and over	48	17	35
GENDER			
Male	42	19	39
Female	42	13	44
DEPARTMENT			
Biological Sciences	35	18	47
Business/Communications	38	17	45
Education	42	16	42
Engineering	42	17	41
Humanities	47	15	38
Mathematics	38	27	36
Physical Sciences	38	22	40
Social Sciences	49	17	34
Other	40	15	45

Table 101

The United States Is Creating an
Overtrained Work Force in Terms of Available Jobs

	AGREE	NEUTRAL	DISAGREE
ALL FACULTY	**20%**	**20%**	**60%**
TYPE OF INSTITUTION			
Four Year	19	20	60
Two Year	21	19	60
CARNEGIE CLASSIFICATION			
Research	15	20	65
Doctorate	21	19	61
Comprehensive	23	21	56
Liberal Arts	20	22	58
Two Year	21	19	60
AGE			
Under 40	19	21	60
40 to 49	18	18	64
50 to 59	21	20	59
60 to 64	18	21	61
65 and over	24	26	50
GENDER			
Male	19	20	61
Female	22	20	58
DEPARTMENT			
Biological Sciences	15	29	56
Business/Communications	19	18	63
Education	21	19	60
Engineering	14	17	70
Humanities	25	23	52
Mathematics	11	19	71
Physical Sciences	11	20	69
Social Sciences	22	20	59
Other	22	15	64

Table 102

Performing Sponsored Research for a Private
Company Is Not a Proper University Activity

	AGREE	NEUTRAL	DISAGREE
ALL FACULTY	**25%**	**19%**	**55%**
TYPE OF INSTITUTION			
Four Year	25	17	58
Two Year	27	23	49
CARNEGIE CLASSIFICATION			
Research	24	16	59
Doctorate	21	14	65
Comprehensive	25	18	57
Liberal Arts	28	23	49
Two Year	27	23	49
AGE			
Under 40	23	19	58
40 to 49	24	17	59
50 to 59	26	23	51
60 to 64	30	17	53
65 and over	34	23	43
GENDER			
Male	25	18	57
Female	27	22	51
DEPARTMENT			
Biological Sciences	20	17	63
Business/Communications	16	19	64
Education	22	20	59
Engineering	14	8	78
Humanities	37	24	39
Mathematics	20	28	52
Physical Sciences	25	13	63
Social Sciences	28	15	57
Other	22	20	58

Table 103

The Abolition of Faculty Tenure Would, on the Whole, Improve the Quality of American Higher Education

	AGREE	NEUTRAL	DISAGREE
ALL FACULTY	**29%**	**12%**	**59%**
TYPE OF INSTITUTION			
Four Year	27	12	60
Two Year	32	12	56
CARNEGIE CLASSIFICATION			
Research	25	12	63
Doctorate	27	13	60
Comprehensive	28	12	60
Liberal Arts	32	14	54
Two Year	32	12	56
AGE			
Under 40	39	14	47
40 to 49	29	12	59
50 to 59	24	12	64
60 to 64	25	13	62
65 and over	25	11	64
GENDER			
Male	27	11	62
Female	32	15	52
DEPARTMENT			
Biological Sciences	26	9	65
Business/Communications	36	11	53
Education	23	14	63
Engineering	35	17	48
Humanities	24	12	64
Mathematics	21	10	69
Physical Sciences	20	9	70
Social Sciences	24	11	64
Other	41	15	45

Table 104

How Would You Characterize Yourself Politically at the Present Time?

	LIBERAL	MODERATELY LIBERAL	MIDDLE-OF-THE-ROAD	MODERATELY CONSERVATIVE	CONSER-VATIVE
ALL FACULTY	**25%**	**32%**	**16%**	**21%**	**6%**
TYPE OF INSTITUTION					
Four Year	29	33	15	18	5
Two Year	19	29	18	26	9
CARNEGIE CLASSIFICATION					
Research	34	33	16	14	3
Doctorate	24	33	15	21	7
Comprehensive	26	33	14	20	7
Liberal Arts	24	35	14	21	6
Two Year	19	29	18	26	9
AGE					
Under 40	30	33	14	15	7
40 to 49	26	34	17	19	4
50 to 59	20	29	15	27	8
60 to 64	23	33	18	20	6
65 and over	31	23	16	22	8
GENDER					
Male	23	31	17	21	7
Female	29	33	14	20	4
DEPARTMENT					
Biological Sciences	26	33	17	17	6
Business/Communications	15	28	17	30	9
Education	23	37	15	22	2
Engineering	13	28	24	29	7
Humanities	36	34	11	13	5
Mathematics	22	29	17	21	11
Physical Sciences	21	33	20	23	3
Social Sciences	34	36	16	12	3
Other	17	27	18	29	10

Chart 40.   I Am Apprehensive About the
                    Future of This Country
                        (percent agreeing)

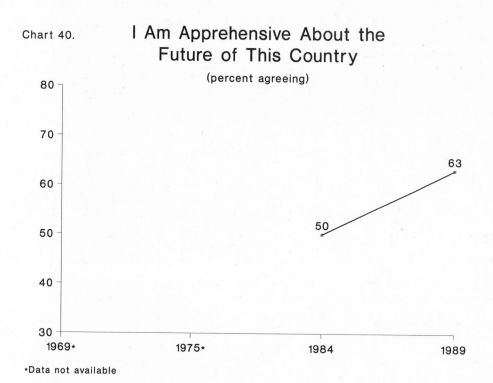

*Data not available

144

APPENDIX A

Technical Notes

Data in this report are derived from The National Survey of Faculty conducted in 1989, and occasionally data from previous surveys.

This most recent survey was conducted for The Carnegie Foundation for the Advancement of Teaching by the Wirthlin Group of McLean, Virginia. A two-stage, stratified, random sample design was used. In the first stage, college and universities were selected; in the second, faculty were designated. For each of the 9 Carnegie Classification types, 34 institutions were selected for a total of 306 colleges and universities. Within each type, an institution was selected with a likelihood proportionate to the size of its faculty compared to the others within that type.

For selecting faculty within the designated colleges and universities, an *n*-th name selection process was used. The 9,996 faculty in the sample were equally divided among Carnegie Classification types. Usable returns numbered 5,450, a 54.5 percent completion rate.

For conducting the analysis, faculty responses were weighted by Carnegie Classification type. The weight used for each type was proportionate to its relative size within the total for all types. Size was defined as the total number of faculty.

The data presented in this publication for the years 1989, 1984, and 1975 are for faculty having full-time appointments. The 1969 data are from all responding faculty.

For several tables in this report, item response categories have been combined as follows: "strongly agree" and "agree with reservations" = "agree"; "strongly disagree" and "disagree with reservations" = "disagree"; "much better" and "somewhat better" = "better"; "much worse" and "somewhat worse" = "worse"; "much higher" and "somewhat higher" = "higher"; "much lower" and "somewhat lower" = "lower"; "a great deal" and "quite a lot" = "a lot."

A P P E N D I X B

Carnegie Classifications

The 1987 Carnegie Classification includes all colleges and universities in the United States listed in the 1985–86 *Higher Education General Information Survey of Institutional Characteristics*. It groups institutions into categories on the basis of the level of degree offered—ranging from prebaccalaureate to the doctorate—and the comprehensiveness of their missions. The categories are as follows:

Research Universities I: These institutions offer a full range of baccalaureate programs, are committed to graduate education through the doctorate degree, and give high priority to research. They receive annually at least $33.5 million in federal support and award at least 50 Ph.D. degrees each year.

Research Universities II: These institutions offer a full range of baccalaureate programs, are committed to graduate education through the doctorate degree, and give high priority to research. They receive annually between $12.5 million and $33.5 million in federal support and award at least 50 Ph.D. degrees each year.

Doctorate-granting Universities I: In addition to offering a full range of baccalaureate programs, the mission of these institutions includes a commitment to graduate education through the doctorate degree. They award at least 40 Ph.D. degrees annually in five or more academic disciplines.

Doctorate-granting Universities II: In addition to offering a full range of baccalaureate programs, the mission of these institutions includes a commitment to graduate education through the doctorate degree. They award annually 20 or more Ph.D. degrees in at least one discipline or 10 or more Ph.D. degrees in three or more disciplines.

Comprehensive Universities and Colleges I: These institutions offer baccalaureate programs and, with few exceptions, graduate education through the master's degree. More than half of their baccalaureate degrees are awarded in two or more occupational or professional disciplines such as engineering or business administration. All of the institutions in this group enroll at least 2,500 students.

Comprehensive Universities and Colleges II: These institutions award more than half of their baccalaureate degrees in two or more occupational or professional disciplines, such as engineering or business administration, and many also offer graduate education through the master's degree. All of the colleges and universities in this group enroll between 1,500 and 2,500 students.

Liberal Arts Colleges I: These highly selective institutions are primarily undergraduate colleges that award more than half of their baccalaureate degrees in art and science fields.

Liberal Arts Colleges II: These institutions are primarily undergraduate colleges that are less selective and award more than half of their degrees in liberal arts fields. This category also includes a group of colleges that award less than half of their degrees in liberal arts fields but, with fewer than 1,500 students, are too small to be considered comprehensive.

Two-Year Community, Junior, and Technical Colleges: These institutions offer certificate or degree programs through the Associate of Arts level and, with few exceptions, offer no baccalaureate degrees.